# Rebirth of Power

Overcoming the Effects
of Sexual Abuse
through the Experiences of Others

edited by
Pamela Portwood, Michele Gorcey
and Peggy Sanders

**illustrated by
Peggy Sanders**

**Published by *Mother Courage Press***

The editors gratefully acknowledge permission to reprint material from the following sources:

Crown Publishers Inc. for material from *Favorite Poems of Emily Dickenson* by Emily Dickenson.

Spinsters/Aunt Lute Book Co. (P.O. Box 410687; San Francisco, CA 94141) for material from the *Cancer Journals* copyright © Audre Lourde.

The editors also acknowledge the publications which first published some of the writings in this collection:

*Agni Review* "What Was It Like, How Does It Feel"
*Convergence* "Rabbit Slaughter"
*Mazagine* "Eleven P.M."
*Quivira* "The Dawning"
*Sinister Wisdom* "Stories My Body Tells"
*Sonoma County Women's Voices* "Old Woman in the Woods"
*Suttertown News* "I Understand Ronald Reagan Because I Understand My Father"
*Woman Spirit* "I am a Woman"

"Spider Monster" copyright © 1987 Stephanie Sugars

---

Library of Congress Catalog Card Number 87-62737
ISBN 0-941300-07-2

Mother Courage Press
1533 Illinois Street
Racine, WI 53405

# Acknowledgments

Over the course of the three years we have spent assembling *Rebirth of Power*, many people helped us in innumerable ways. We would like to express our gratitude to all of them.

First, we would like to thank the authors, both for their courageous writings and for their patience through this long process. We also are grateful to the many other authors whose work we could not include in the anthology but who shared their personal and moving writings with us.

The following women and organizations helped us solicit work, proof the writings and publicize the project: Karen Brown, Coordinating Committee on Sexual and Domestic Violence; Nancy Douglas-Payne, Ellen, Roni Kendall, Kino Community Hospital's Department of Psychiatry; Lisa Lahaie, Susan Patania, Pegasis Touch, Tucson Rape Crisis Center and Tucson Women's Alliance. Barbara Lindquist of Mother Courage Press has been enthusiastic about this project from our first correspondence, and her sensitivity has cushioned the publishing process.

Although the creation of *Rebirth of Power* has been a collective project, we, as editors, each would like to thank those people who have sustained us individually throughout this process.

I, Pamela, would like to thank Mark Taylor, my husband, for his steadfast support, understanding and love through my personal healing process and through the long commitment of completing this anthology. Also, my friends Jan Bowers, Barbara Kingsolver and Jeanne Taylor have been continuing inspirations to me as a writer and a survivor of sexual assault.

I, Michele, wish to thank the many courageous rape and incest survivors who spent hours with me sharing their abuse experiences. It was through this sharing (my research) that I met my co-editors and recognized the value of writing as healing. Also, my many friends, my family and Kenny provided me with their continual support, encouragement and love.

For helping me get to this point, I, Peggy, wish to thank Carol DeLuca, who was an inspiration to me; my family and friends, who were always there for me in difficult times; Las Familias—in particular Adults Molested As Children—for shedding light on terribly private issues for many bewildered individuals and for helping me on the path to healing; and John, who believed in me.

# Introduction

*Rebirth of Power: Overcoming the Effects of Sexual Abuse through the Experiences of Others* seeks to shatter the silence which preserves and condones sexual violence in our society. Happily, more and more is being written and televised about sexual assault. Yet too often, the issue remains at a distance, stereotyped as something that perverse strangers do to other people's children and to women out alone at night. Still, too little has reached the public about the actual experience and its aftermath in the individual survivor's life—one, two . . . twenty, thirty years later. Too often, even those involved with the issues of sexual assault have shied away from examining the frightening roots of sexual violence in our society.

*Rebirth of Power* seeks to break the stereotypes and illusions surrounding sexual assault by providing space for those most qualified to address the issue to share the knowledge they have gained at painful prices. The survivors are the ones who know what it means to be raped by a relative, friend or stranger. They know what a lifetime of silence about incest can do to a person's psyche. Theirs are the voices which can compel us to understand, to care and to do something about sexual violence.

This collection reflects the pervasiveness of sexual abuse. It includes accounts of women, children and men who have been assaulted by fathers, stepfathers, grandfathers, brothers, uncles, husbands, mothers, neighbors, friends of the family, friends of the survivor, strangers, gangs of inmates and of teenagers. The writings show how rapists cross all socio-economic brackets and professions from gardener to doctor to minister. And the survivors speak not only of the actual assault but of society's subsequent mental rape: the lack of belief and support by family members, the sometimes misguided help of social service workers, the inadequacies of our legal system and people's unwillingness, in general, to deal with the pain of others.

But mostly *Rebirth of Power* reveals the long, hard return to an integrated self after the violation. Organized into the three sections of "Experiences," "Consequences" and "Healing," the anthology offers other survivors a spectrum of places in which to enter, to see themselves more clearly through the lives of others who have endured similar experiences, to find ways of coping with the trauma's aftermath in their lives. For professionals, the writings provide more contact with the lives and problems of survivors as well as with specific techniques which helped them learn to thrive in their lives. For the public in general, these are stories to remember, lives by which to be moved, and they proffer the realities of sexual abuse directly, creatively, unemcumbered by commentary or jargon. Also, the resource material at the end of the book provides a general guide to finding help, nationwide, with the issues of sexual assault.

To an extent, dividing the work into the categories of experiences, consequences and healing is fallacious. It suggests that the healing process is essentially linear and can be handled in discreet, manageable units. This is not the case, nor do we, as editors, mean to imply that those whose writings are included in the first two sections are not "healed." The healing process is a continuum that begins the moment after the assault: simply living through it means stepping onto the continuum. For us, organizing the writings by stages in the healing process affirms, first and foremost, that there is hope. Survivors can and have entered those experiences consciously, grappled with the feelings, screamed at the rapists, disowned the guilt, validated their lives, integrated the entire process into the self and emerged as whole and stronger human beings.

Although healing processes, like assault experiences, vary from person to person, a commonality underscores them all. This commonality arises from the fact that sexual assault, regardless of the form it takes or the relationship of the assailant to the survivor, involves one person's abuse of unequal power to violate the body, mind and spirit of another. The heart of sexual assault is not sex but violence and power. Born of the inequities of a patriarchal culture, sexual assault is primarily a violent expression of male domination over the disempowered members of our society—typically women and children. Men too are raped, but they are abused most commonly by other men and abused at times and in places where they have become powerless, namely as children and adolescents and in jails. Periodically, women are abusers, but they are the exceptions.

Although the details of assault experiences are unique in the individual circumstance, many of the same consequences recur: feelings of guilt and of responsibility for the assault; the loss of self esteem; a fear of intimacy; an inability to trust others; ambivalent feelings about one's sexuality and one's sexual identity; feelings of powerlessness and of loss of control over one's life; generalized feelings of depression, fear and anxiety, even terror.[1] Yet at last, these long-term consequences of sexual assault are not being written off by the medical profession and by society at large as something survivors should simply "get over." At last, these consequences are being acknowledged, validated and even classified as "post-traumatic stress disorder."[2]

These consequences emerge from the powerful and destructive messages of abuse: you are unworthy and less than a person; you are at fault for a powerlessness imposed from without; you are not entitled to power over your own body or life; if you are trusting or vulnerable, you risk being abused. What silence preserves among survivors is a sense of isolation: something so terrible could not possibly have happened to anyone else; no one else could have such bad and guilty feelings; no one would understand. Reading the experiences of others reveals how these feelings do not arise from within the self but are imposed falsely from without by a society which typically will not discuss or face up to the realities of rape in its many manifestations.

The taboo is not on incest or rape because they are too common; the taboo is on speaking about incest, rape and any form of sexual assault. Thirty-eight percent of all women interviewed by Diana Russell in a door-to-door study of a general population in San Francisco reported at least one experience of intrafamilial or extrafamilial sexual abuse before the age of eighteen.[3] In Mary Koss' recent study, 40 percent of college women and 44 percent of adult women stated they had been victims of rape or attempted rape.[4] Estimates of the number of sexual assaults which go unreported vary from 50 to 90 percent.[5] The combined statistics of these and other studies make it not unreasonable to expect that perhaps half of all American women will experience some form of sexual violence in their lifetime.

Heretofore, studies have shown between one in ten and one in five American men were sexually assaulted as children.[6] However, based on numerous citations, studies and interviews, Fay Honey Knopp supports the theory that male children are at equal or near-equal risk of being sexually victimized as female children are. While the overwhelming majority of girls are victimized by a male family member or a male family acquaintance, Knopp indicates that boys are most often abused by men outside the home.[7] Although Eugene Porter estimates only a small percentage of male victims become perpetrators, he cites Knopp's studies which have shown that up to 100% of incarcerated perpetrators who have committed the severest sexual abuses were sexually victimized as children.[8] Clearly, the early detection and treatment of sexually abused boys is an important link in the prevention of all forms of sexual assault.

Sexual abuse is not a perverse idiosyncrasy of our time; it is woven warp and weft into the very fabric of our culture. For example, the Talmud asserts that a girl who is three years and one day old may be betrothed by sexual intercourse, provided her father has given consent.[9] In the early Hebrew tradition, sex with a girl under the age of three was not illegal, merely invalid; in the early Christian tradition, the age for such invalid sex was seven.[10] Historically, our culture has defined women and children as the property of men, and today sexual abuse is a sometime overt, sometimes insidious, way of preserving that balance of power. Rape is an oppressor's tool for keeping the disenfranchised members of a society disenfranchised. Ultimately, countering sexual violence means examining and changing our very notions of what it means to be men, women and children in our culture.

The writers in *Rebirth of Power* assert that as survivors we will not be silent or be silenced any longer. For many of us, writing—poems, journal entries, stories, fables, sent and unsent letters—has been the saving grace. When spoken words were too frightening, pen and paper became our tongues. When our psyches protected us from our memories, our poems and dream journals spoke them symbolically for us. Sometimes our writings recorded our healing process; sometimes they actually created the process and the means.

We have saved ourselves through a myriad of methods: rituals, dreams, myths, anger, political action, therapy, support groups, spirituality, feminist analysis and, of course, love. We have beaten pillows, hugged dolls, prayed and meditated. We literally have gone into the wilderness. In speaking our past, we have usurped its power and freed ourselves. We have reclaimed our bodies, our selves, our childhoods and even our very lives from those who raped us.

What living through sexual assault and its aftermath has

taught us invariably is that we can endure and survive anything. But we will not excuse, romanticize or ignore sexual violence in our lives or in our society. In speaking the truths of our individual lives, we make the truths of sexual assault on a social scale known. In facing our personal pain, we have found the courage to speak out, and in speaking out, we endeavor to change the world even as we have changed ourselves, piece by piece, one small step at a time.

Pamela Portwood
Tucson, Arizona

[1] Jose M. Santiago, M.D., Fred McCall-Perez, Ph.D., Michele Gorcey, M.S.W. and Allan Beigel, M.D., "Long-term Psychological Effects of Rape," *American Journal of Psychiatry*, 142 (November 1985), 1338-1340.

[2] M. Gorcey, J. Santiago and F. McCall-Perez, "Psychological Consequences for Women Sexually Abused in Childhood," *Social Psychiatry*, 21 (1986), 129-133.

[3] D. Russell, "The incidence and prevalence of intrafamilial sexual abuse of children," *Child Abuse and Neglect*, 7 (1983), 133-146.

[4] M. P. Koss, "The scope of rape," *The Clinical Psychologist*, Summer 1983, p. 90.

[5] Data suggesting that only 40 to 50 percent of rapes committed are reported to the police is from the Law Enforcement Assistance Administration, *Criminal Victimization Surveys in 13 American Cities* (Washington, D.C.: U.S. Government Printing Office, 1975), n. pag. The 90 percent estimate for non-reporting of sexual assaults is from the pamphlet: Women Against Rape, *The Assault Prevention Training Project* (Columbus, Ohio: Women Against Rape, n.d.), n. pag.

[6] In David Finkelhor's study, 8.6 percent of the college-age males interviewed had been sexually assaulted as children; almost none of them revealed the abuse at the time. See Finkelhor, *Sexually Victimized Children* (New York: Free Press, 1979), p. 53.

[7] Fay Honey Knopp, "Introduction" to Eugene Porter, M.A., *Treating the Young Male Victim of Sexual Assault: Issues & Intervention Stategies* (New York: Safer Society Press, 1986), pp. 1-11. Statistics on the victimization of girls can be found in M. Gorcey, p. 130.

[8] Knopp and Porter, pp. 14-32. Both Knopp and Porter also deal with the problems arising for boy victims as a consequence of the

social stigmas attached to homosexuality and of the sex-role stereotypes of males as the sexually aggressive partners in heterosexual relationships (pp. 10-13, 29-36).

[9] Seder Nezikin, ed., *The Babylonian Talmud*, trans. I. Epstein (London: The Soncino Press, 1935), p. 376, as quoted in Florence Rush, *The Best Kept Secret: Sexual Abuse of Children* (New York: McGraw-Hill, 1980), p. 18.

[10] Rush, p. 34.

# Contents

## Experiences

## Consequences

# Experiences

# daddy's good little girl

he pins her head
to the dirty, white, one-inch tiled
bathroom floor.
takes out mommy's red
lip stick
and it breaks in half
as he smears it over her mouth.
   her head twists
back and forth
     her protests are sounds
like blood gurgling from a throat
wound.

but that only allows him to get some
lip stick on her teeth.

then he smiles at her
clowned mouth.
his power holds her

still. her lipsticked mouth is a wound
   he sucks then smears he sucks then smears

further by his

kiss.


**Jane Doe #1**: i am twenty-four. a textile artist/sculptor. a libra. i have survived mother/daughter incest with the help of: music, art, poetry, Goddess, candlelit baths and two therapists. i now live in california with my partner and my cat, Kharma. i finally know why it is worth it to survive.

there are times when my heart sings, my body trembles so full of light and potential that i feel i might open the window and drift upwards on a warm californian breeze.

# Spider Monster

The leaves had fallen from the oak tree out front of the school. Days were dawning a little darker. Cold was wrapping its arms around the school yard.

During art class, the first graders drew five-finger turkeys, coloring in each tail feather of the turkey a different color. The teacher had a stencil for the wattles and comb which the children took turns tracing onto red construction paper.

After she'd cut them with round scissors and glued them down with white paste, she sat and looked at the oak balls on the tree. Her friend Molly said spiders lived in those oak balls and planted their eggs in them. She didn't care about spiders, just about the way the brown balls looked against the gray sky.

Her grandma and grandpa came today. Tomorrow they would stay home and eat. She liked the way those oak balls looked. She'd remember them for tomorrow. It worked sometimes. If she'd remember something really well, then she wouldn't think about what was going to happen tomorrow.

Finally everyone else got their turkeys finished. The teacher had them clean up their desks. When the bell rang, they were all standing in line to leave, coats buttoned to the throat, hands full of turkey and wide-lined paper.

She was sad to go home. It didn't seem right. Surely the order at school should stay all around her. Surely she should know. After all, her mama said she was a big girl, six years old. She thought about it a lot, dragging the toe of her sneaker through the gutter. "I otta know, I otta know. All about this, all about this. What's a kiss, what's a kiss? How about it, how about it?"

There was something she otta know. It looked like an oak ball swaying in the wind. It looked like the fingers of her hand turning into a turkey's tail. It smelled like mildew-damp places. She otta know. She smelt the smoke from the burning leaves, felt the water pushing into her tennis shoe.

It was sad going home. Something very sad would happen and

no one would talk about it. She would try to remember about how to button a coat and which way her shoes laced up. She would think about burning leaves, not mildew. She would see oak trees not her grandfather's eyes as they rushed to gobble her up. She thought she was chewing on a crayon or a piece of chalk not anything soft. Not any big Thanksgiving meal.

Her mother yelled at her for getting her shoes muddy. Then her grandpa came into the kitchen and said, "How's my little girl?" He took her to play in the living room.

Something big and soft tried to get into bed with her. She thought it was the turkey neck coming out of the middle of the turkey. It was squishy poking her arm.

Waking up she thought there was something she was going to remember, something she otta know. This must be a time when she was going to remember something else. But she forgot and opened her eyes. There was a monster next to her. It looked like her grandpa but it was really big. She wondered if a spider lived inside her grandpa's body. A spider monster jumping out of his eyes onto her face. A spider monster crawling under her p.j.'s. A spider monster jerking his body around.

Then she remembered. The oak balls. Oh yes, how they looked on the tree like decorations against the gray sky. And it was funny the way Molly said her name, Molly Tamale while kicking her holey shoes against the steel-mesh fence. She liked school. Grown-ups were nice there every day, not just some days. She thought about the crayons and how they felt between her fingers, like turkey feathers rubbing soft.

The spider monster was rubbing hard now, pressing her legs close together around that big thing that grew out of its stomach. Sometimes the spider monster's big thing grew really hard, then it spit gray stuff onto her. Other times it was soft and pressed hard on her. It made her skin all itchy. Sometimes it went really hard into her mouth. Tonight, because it was Thanksgiving, she thought she was eating an oak ball. The spider was planting it in her mouth. It kept pushing the oak ball in deep so she would swallow it. Dumb monster, didn't it know that she never could swallow it yet?

Something really sad was happening, and she couldn't remember everything she was going to remember. Tomorrow they were going to gobble up the gobbler. That's what her dad said.

Tonight though her ears were full of hard spider eggs. They hurt from where her mouth was all opened up for the monster thing. Everything she could hear was hard and thick. This must be what it's like when a monster comes and you get too scared to run away. Pretty soon it would stop, like it always did, pretty soon. Not soon enough. The monster held on for just a little more, then it stiffened up and that big thing got squishy and mildew spit out of it.

Her grandpa came back then. He patted her head and told her she was a good girl who loved him so much more than anything in the world. He told her he loved her back more than anything in the world too. And that she'd always be his little girl. She couldn't hear because the thing in her throat had made her ears swell closed. And she was glad she couldn't hear. Even though the monsters were sad and scary, they weren't as bad as the after time with her grandfather.

Pretty soon he left after putting his tongue against hers.

She remembered that today she colored a turkey, got her tennis shoes wet in the gutter, saw those oak balls, how pretty they looked on the tree. She remembered when she got home that her mom must have hugged her and said hi. That was all. The hurt in her ears shrunk up to dry egg cases. That was all. No spider monsters. No grandpa. The oak balls stayed on the tree. No turkey tomorrow. That was all. She otta know.

**Stephanie Sugars**: "Spider Monster" is a semi-autobiographical story. As a child, magic and mystery became explanations for abhorrent adult behavior. Speaking out about fifteen years of incestuous assault is an answering of riddles created to protect myself in childhood. Now adult life is a joy and delight. My deepening appreciation of the world's mysteries provides inspiration and courage to carry on.

# Ten Forty-Four

They say I look at them
with eyes iced-over, hiding,
offering nothing.
I'm telling you, it wasn't always like that.

This is what happened:
on the hottest day of August,
one of those when the sun
fills the skin, like a leaf,
I was working in my garden,
rows of bean, rows of lettuce.
A man came to the house.
A well-dressed, regular type,
polite enough, in trouble,
said his car broke down.
He didn't look too well and maybe
needed to get in
out of the sun.
He asked if he could
ask me for a favor.
In those days it was my habit
to say I would,
even before I asked,
"What do you want?"
He followed me in.
I poured water in a china cup,
*china,*
for this man,
and then he asked
if I would do just one more thing.
I felt, before I saw it,
the stainless point shoved between the ribs,
dead center on the heartbeat
I had learned to treasure

for so many years.
A treasure in a cage
so easily opened.
I said,
"Yes I will."
I didn't ask, "What is it
that you want?"
That was the last time.

There are things that cannot be felt
in imagination,
only in skin and blood.
That was my own knife.
I had used it on a hundred
ordinary days
to peel my vegetables,
and with the same regard for me
he used it,
peeled off dignity,
love for solitude,
trust.

The officers came promptly
as if they had been waiting.
They fingerprinted everything
including me and stated
endlessly into their open radios
that there had been a ten forty-four
on 12th street.
That's what they called it.
These grown men who carry guns
could not bring themselves to call by name
what had been done to me.
Instead they gathered traces,
from my body,
from the broken cup, things
that could not have been more empty,
they collected what they needed.
A trace of hair or blood or sperm

to bring him down.
The hunt
was what mattered.

They didn't
ever find him.  And strangely,
my fear takes other forms.
I don't expect him back,
because he's finished here.
No silver under the bed,
no valuables to come back for.
Especially,
not trust.
I keep it in a locked drawer with my kitchen knives
and other things of mine that have been used against me.

January 1981

**Barbara Kingsolver:** I spent years refusing to think about my sexual assault before finally letting myself feel the extent of the injury, and grieve.  Over several months I faced my pain and, through reading, writing and talking, developed a perspective that helped me get on with my life.  These writings are part of that recovery.

By profession I'm a writer concerned with women's issues and struggles for social change; my articles, fiction, and poetry appear in various magazines.  My novel, *The Bean Trees*, will be released by Harper and Row in 1988.  Like every writer, I work from my own experience—in my case this includes considerable anger, love, and the certainty that change is possible.

# Lessons

It was dry. It hadn't rained in four weeks and it was dry. The earth lay cracked and open in the fields and the land coughed up its discontent in dust. Celie looked out of her bedroom window at the sky lying low and mean against the horizon. There were clouds, but she didn't know if they would bring rain. The man on the radio said they might, but the man on the radio had been saying that for a week and a half.

She sighed and got up from her seat by the window. She had to get dressed. Momma'd be calling her soon, for it was Sunday and she had to go to church. On Wednesday nights there was Bible study and on Thursday nights there were prayer meetings. Now it was Sunday and she had to go to church. She didn't see why they had to go again.

"Because we have to. That's why," her mother would say. But Celie didn't get it, didn't see why it was so important. The Bible said to honor the Sabbath day, not every day. Like the Catholics. They went to church once a week and had the rest of the week off. She wasn't going to ask Momma about it, though. No sir. You got the back of a hand when you asked too many questions. Celie knew all about that.

She pulled her pink dress with the lace collar over her head and down around her hips. She hated that dress. It was too small for her and too little girl looking. Her grandma had made it for her three Christmases ago when she was twelve. She'd grown a lot in two years. She needed a new dress. One that was green, she thought, and pictured herself in a green dress with little flowers on it. She'd seen some material over at the T.G.& Y. and knew just how she'd make it. It'd have long sleeves and a narrow skirt and a nice wide belt so she could show off her waist. It would have a pretty neckline with a white collar. Oh, what she wouldn't give for a white grown-up collar. Momma just didn't understand.

"Celie," she'd say. "Celie, you need to quit thinkin' on such things. It's the devil at work, it is, and you'd better watch it. As the Good Book says, '... the woman was arrayed in purple and scarlet

10

colour, and decked with gold and precious stones and pearls, having a golden cup in her hand full of abominations and filthiness of her fornication.' Don't you go gettin' no abominations or fornicatin' now."

Celie was awfully tired of hearing that. Awfully tired. Lord, help me, she thought, to remember You in my true need but if I could have a green dress with little flowers on it like over at the T.G.&Y. and if it could have a pretty neckline and a real grown-up collar, I'd be forever grateful, yes I would. Amen.

She heard her brother Jess starting up the car. The horn honked and her Momma called, "Celie, you come on now," and with a last tug at the skirt of the pink dress, she ran out of the house, down the steps, and out to the car. As she got in, her mother turned around and looked at her sharply. "Girl, you think all we got to do is wait on the likes of you to get ready, primpin' in front of the mirror? Huh? Now where's your hat? You cain't go into a house of God without a hat."

"Oh, I'll get it real fast, Momma, I promise." And she was out of the car. She ran into the house and straight to her bedroom. Now where was it? She threw open the closet door. Jess honked the horn. Momma called, "Celie?"

"Damn," she said, and putting her hand to her mouth, she stopped. What had she done? She could hear her Momma's voice saying "... no abominations, do you hear?" "Oh, Lord, forgive me my iniquity," she said, and breathed a sigh of relief when she saw her hat hanging on the chair next to the window. She grabbed it and ran out of the house, slamming the door behind her.

The drive to the church was long. Long and hot. Celie looked at the creepers and bushes drooping on the side of the road. A thin layer of dust covered the leaves, coloring them a strange shade neither brown nor green but somewhere in between.

"You know," Jess said, "we don't get us some rain real soon and we can say good-bye to the crop. Momma, Celie May, y'all better pray for some rain today."

"His will be done, Jess," Momma said.

"Yes, Ma'am. I suppose it will anyhow."

Celie looked out of the window at the flat land that stretched out away in the distance as far as she could see. Nothing broke the long flat line of the horizon. Not a hill, not a tree. It was like a razor slicing across her vision. She turned her gaze away from it.

"Momma," she said, pulling her skirt down around her knees for what seemed like the hundredth time. "Momma, I'm gonna have to get a new dress." Her mother turned around in the front seat to look at her.

"Why?" she wanted to know.

"Oh, Momma, I hate this dress. Look at it. It's old and ugly and besides, I cain't hardly fit in it anymore."

"You were mighty glad to get it when Grandma first gave it to you."

Celie said nothing while her mother shook her head.

"Celie, the devil's gettin' to you. There ain't nothin' wrong with that dress. It's been fine all this time. How come you just startin' to complain now?"

"It's how girls are, Momma," Jess said. "Celie May's gettin' to that age where all she's gonna think about is clothes and boys and you'd best start watchin' her. First thing you know she'll be expectin' and where'll you be? A grandma yourself, that's where."

"Jess, you just shut up," Celie cried. "I ain't that kinda girl. You ought to know that. Momma's raised me better'n that."

Momma said, "Celie, don't talk to your brother that way, do you hear?" Celie didn't say anything and Momma turned toward her son. "Jess, I think I know how girls are. In case you've forgotten, I used to be one."

He looked over at her. "Oh, well, Momma, I didn't mean—"

She smiled. "I know you didn't, Son," and she patted his knee. Jess covered her little hand with his and squeezed it. They smiled at each other.

Their hands remained together a long time, Celie thought. She backed away from the picture they made, retreated into the rear seat, cut off, shut out from what was happening. Again. She turned away from it back to the horizon. Her eyes burned and she blinked angrily. She wasn't going to cry. She wouldn't. If she cried, they would really start to pick on her. She wished she had somebody to be on her side. It hadn't been like this when Daddy was alive. He had always been on her side and they had always won. After he'd died, though, things had been different. That had been two years ago and ever since then Jess could do anything he wanted and Momma wouldn't take up for her.

"Seems like you need to be taught a lesson, Celie, honey," he'd say and he'd come for her. Once she had run away, but when he'd caught her, it had only been that much worse. Jess was twenty-five years old. What could she do to make him leave her alone if he didn't want to? Momma didn't help at all. The first time it had happened, he hadn't really made her do anything. But the times since then it had been worse. She had finally gone to Momma and tried to tell her, but Momma hadn't believed her.

"What do you mean sayin' things like that about your brother? Your own flesh and blood?" she'd hissed. "Just what do you mean?" And Momma had laid the back of her hand across Celie's face. No, she couldn't tell Momma.

They were almost at church. She could see the cars lined up in the dusty parking lot. There was Rose Beckinaw, her best friend, and she—why she—Celie's attention was riveted to her dress. She wouldn't—oh yes, she would and she had. Rose's dress was just like the one Celie had wanted. The one with little white flowers on it. The one with the narrow waist. It even had the grown-up white collar. Why, Rose must have gone to the T.G.& Y. the same day Celie had told her about it. Celie stared with an open mouth as Jess pulled into the parking lot and stopped the car. How could she? Celie thought.

"Celie May," said Jess, already out of the car and opening her door and their Momma's door at the same time. "Celie May, you come on out now and close your mouth. You look just like that little Kinchen girl what ain't got no brains."

Celie didn't even look at her brother standing outside the car. She was busy watching as Rose turned and saw her and then hurried after her father into church.

"In a minute," she said.

"You'll come now," Jess said and yanked her out of the back seat. "You know, Celie, honey," he said in her ear as he pushed her up behind Momma, "seems like you need another lesson."

"You better not, Jess," she hissed.

"Oh, yeah? And who's gonna stop me?" he laughed low behind her ear and pinched her. Jess had a way of pinching where he'd grab the skin on her arm and twist at the same time. It hurt. A lot. Celie threw her arm back and caught the side of his face with her hand. The motion surprised her. She wasn't used to hitting her brother. It surprised him, too. His head jerked up. Momma turned around.

"What on earth is wrong with you two? Acting like you're two years old, both of you. Now behave." And she strode into the church ahead of them.

"That's gonna cost you, Sugar," Jess said and he smiled. But the smile only touched his mouth. It didn't go anywhere near his eyes. "Yessir," he said again. "Gonna cost you a lot." He held the door open for her to go inside. Celie stood still a moment looking up at her brother. "Go on in," he said and she did. Momma had gotten a seat way in the front so she had to walk all the way up there in that silly pink dress with her brother following quietly behind her. She slid in next to Momma when she got to the pew and Jess sat down next to her but far enough away so he wasn't touching her at all.

Celie didn't know what to do. Jess looked real funny. What was worse, he felt real funny to her. The dumb smile was still on his mouth, but his eyes stared straight ahead. He didn't say anything to her or Momma. He didn't even look at them. Celie thought about when they would go home. That was the thing. She hoped that maybe Momma would stay home today and not go visit anywhere and then after a while, Jess wouldn't be mad anymore and look so funny.

The preacher came out shortly after they sat down. Celie barely had time to say a prayer before they had to stand up and sing the first song. She thought Preacher Thompson looked mad today, so he'd probably talk a long time. That was good. Give her a chance to think. Jess wouldn't dare do anything if Momma was around. The problem was if Momma left. She always went to her room and locked her door to get away from Jess when Momma left. A couple of times, though, she'd gone to the room after Momma drove off to find him waiting for her behind the door and he'd grabbed her and said, "It's time for a lesson, Celie May," and then he'd made her do things. She closed her eyes and tried not to think. Maybe if Momma went off this afternoon, she'd let her go along. Yeah, maybe she'd do that.

The song ended and Preacher Thompson began to speak. Celie liked to listen to him talk. He always got so excited. Especially when he was mad. His face would get red and a sheen would glisten as he began to sweat. His voice would start off slow and easy like when it rained in the spring and then it would begin to fall harder and harder till it pounded into their ears like the thunder and lightning that Preacher Thompson said was the wrath of God.

She turned her head slightly to look at her brother. The smile had

14

gone from his face and left a thin line that looked like a crack in cement in the place where his mouth was supposed to be.

He still would not look at her.

Off to her left she could see Rose Beckinaw in that green dress and she hated her, hated her white skin that looked so nice next to the dark green, hated the blond hair, hated the slender body and thought, "Rose Beckinaw, I'll never speak to you again, I won't, and you look like a fat green cow!" But she didn't feel any better and, opening her Bible, she set it carefully on her lap.

"The Lord knows a sinner," Preacher Thompson was saying matter of factly. "A man who used to beat his wife every day came to me and said, 'Preacher, I beat my wife and I'd like to stop.' And I said to him, I said, 'Sinner, cast this demon from you for a wife's a fine thing and ought not to be abused.'"

The women in the church nodded their heads vigorously. "Amen, Preacher!" called the lady sitting behind Celie. "Praise the Lord," said the lady on the other side of Jess. Preacher Thompson continued.

"Now I saw this woman and she was pretty. Real pretty. Her husband said he hated the way other men looked at his wife and he wanted to make them quit so he used to black her eyes and fatten her lips so she wouldn't be near as pretty. And I told him, I said, 'Sinner, the Lord knows a fool and will treat him accordingly. He, in His wisdom, made your wife a pretty woman and you've no right to go makin' ugly that which the Lord has decided will be pretty. Therefore, you must not beat your wife.' And the man went and raised up his wife and said, 'Woman, be glad, for I shall not beat you any longer since the Lord knows a fool.' And to this day, the man has not laid a hand upon her."

"Hallelujah, Brother!" cried the woman in the row behind them. "The Lord knows a fool, yes He does." "Praise His name!" cried a man in the back of the church.

Celie sat transfixed by the preacher. "The Lord knows a fool," she thought, and looked over at Jess. Then she looked at the Bible lying on her lap and she placed her hand carefully along the center. "He won't hurt me today," she thought. "I swear. Today I'm not going to let him hurt me."

She hoped he had listened to the preacher. She hoped he had paid close attention. She didn't want to have to mess with him for the Lord knew, he was a fool.

15

The rest of the sermon flew by. Preacher Thompson was saying something about adultery, but Celie didn't hear it. She kept thinking about the Lord knowing fools. When it was over, she got up to sing the final hymn and followed Momma and Jess out the door. The sky had clouded over during the service and the wind was picking up.

"Praise the Lord," Jess said. "The crop won't be ruined."

"Yes. Praise His name," Momma agreed. "You know, I believe I'll go over to Maggie's for the afternoon after all, Jess. You can drop me off on the way home."

"Momma, can I go with you?"

Momma turned and looked at Celie. "Now what on earth do you want to go for?" She shook her head. "No, you go on home with your brother and fix him something to eat for dinner."

"But, Momma—"

"No, Celie." And Momma turned around.

It was then that the rain broke, pattering into the dust lying thickly on the ground, sending up miniature dust devils every time a drop exploded into the powdery gray-brown. They all rushed to the car and jumped in, beating the storm just in time before the water streamed down from the sky. Jess started up the old Buick and drove out of the parking lot.

When they were nearing Maggie Goodman's house, a little over half the way home, Momma turned around. "Now, Celie? You behave yourself and mind your brother, you hear?"

She tied her hat firmly under her chin so the rain wouldn't mess her hair. Celie didn't know why her Momma insisted on wearing those old ugly hats she'd had forever. They weren't white trash. She didn't see why Momma had to dress like they were. The door opened and slammed quickly as Momma got out of the car. Jess smiled and waved good-bye to his mother, then pressed the accelerator.

"You heard what Momma said, Celie May? You heard her, huh?"

Celie didn't say anything. She just looked at the side of the road and the fields passing by so swiftly.

"You hear me, girl?" Jess said and grabbed her arm.

She shook herself free. "Jess, slow down. You gonna have us in the ditch if you don't drive slower."

"Well, yes Ma'am," he said and slowed the car down. "I surely

16

do want to get home safe because the Lord knows we got things to do you and me." And he smiled.

Celie stared at the road ahead and said nothing. She didn't get it. When she had been real little, Jess used to look out for her. Once after school when she was in first grade and Peggy Becker and Bobby Mason were picking on her, he had come and made them leave her alone. She didn't know what he'd said to them, but they'd never bothered her again.

She leaned her head against the window. It was when she'd turned fourteen that it had all changed. She just didn't understand. Jess was a good-looking guy. He could probably have just about any girl he wanted. But he didn't date anyone. He used to, but he'd stopped when she'd turned fourteen. He'd taken her out to the barn and that's when it had happened the first time.

She turned her head away from the window quickly, snapping it almost, to the road ahead of her. She wouldn't think about that now. She needed to figure out a way to keep him from doing it again.

They were home almost before she knew it, though she was aware with each passing mile of the fact that they were getting closer to the house. She had never felt this way before. As though her insides were almost burning.

Jess pulled up to the front door in the still dusty yard. The rain had not yet reached their land. The car stopped before the porch with a lurch and Jess turned off the motor. He turned to her and smiled.

"Come on, Celie May," he said. "Let's go inside and you can fix me somethin' to eat." He opened his door and got out of the car. Celie sat still in the car, watching him. He didn't stop and wait for her but walked up the steps, over the porch, and into the house. He sure seemed easy for somebody who'd been so mad just a little while ago.

She looked to the right of the house over to the barn. She thought about the hay up in the loft. She could go up there but that probably wouldn't be any good. She guessed Jess would just follow her up there and at least in the house she'd have a chance. She wished she could go to the barn and lie hidden in the hay somewhere, smelling its sweetness like she used to do when she was little. But she couldn't. She didn't even really like the barn now. She only liked the memory of it, the way it was, the way it used to be.

17

She stopped herself. She took a deep breath and got out of the car. She stood still a moment and looked at the screen door. She wondered if he thought she was stupid. He had done this to her once before. She walked cautiously up the steps and onto the porch so her shoes wouldn't make any noise. The front door wasn't open all the way, so she looked to the side by the opening and then through the crack to see if he was hiding behind the door. She jumped when he spoke.

"Girl, what are you doin'?" He was standing in the hallway. "Here I'm starving half to death and you're playing games with the door. Will you get in the kitchen and fix us somethin' to eat? Damn." And he turned and went into the bathroom. She heard the door shut and then the sound of running water.

Celie walked to her room quickly and locked the door behind her. Unhooking the collar of the dress and reaching behind her head, she pulled it up and over her shoulders and off. She hung it in the closet behind her winter coat and walked over to her dresser for jeans and an old shirt. A knock at the door made her turn quickly.

"Celie May?"

She grabbed a shirt out of the drawer and pulled it over her head. "What?" she said.

"You almost done? I'm hungry."

She pulled on her jeans. "I'm coming," she said. "Besides, what's wrong with you? You crippled? Fix yourself some crackers or somethin' till dinner's ready. It's gonna take a minute."

"Well, hurry up." He twisted the knob. "What you got this door locked for? Huh, Celie May? You afraid somethin's gonna happen?" She heard him walk away laughing. She could see him laughing, his dark head thrown back, his white, even teeth. He could have any girl he wanted.

She brushed her hair and set the brush down on the dresser. There was a fine tracing of gray in the corners by the mirror. She was going to have to dust. Her lip curled as she ran a finger on the surface, leaving a clean streak in its wake. She hated to dust.

"Celie May!" Jess called.

He was standing in the kitchen, staring into the open refrigerator when she walked in. "There ain't nothin' to eat," he said when he saw her. She rolled her eyes. He always said that.

"Don't you roll your eyes at me, girl." He spun around quickly.

He took a step toward her "Don't you ever roll your eyes at me."

She swallowed. There was something in her throat. The look was in his eyes again. She swallowed a second time, but the thing in her throat wouldn't go away. He had her cornered. He started to move toward her again, but stopped. His eyes changed. He laughed. "I'm hungry, honey," he said. "You gonna fry that chicken Momma left out?"

It didn't take long to fix the food, but it didn't matter since Celie wasn't very hungry. She looked at Jess' face as he ate, but he was busy filling his mouth. She looked at his shoulders and thought about the muscles underneath the fabric of his shirt. He was strong, she knew. She had seen him bend a metal bar once with only his hands. "Just for fun," he'd said. She looked back at his face and saw that he was looking at her. He wiped his mouth with the back of his hand and smiled slowly.

She sat very still in her chair. That look was back. He was looking at her that *way* again. She couldn't stand that look. She had to do something.

"You done eatin'?" she said and stood up. But Jess didn't say anything. "Well, gotta do the dishes," she said. "You just go ahead and finish. I'm going to the bathroom. Be back in a minute." She walked out of the kitchen and heard him get up directly, pushing his chair back from the table, and as he did, the wood scraping grudgingly against the floor. She began to run and made it to the front door. He hadn't locked it. Why hadn't he locked it?

"Oh, Lord," she prayed, "let me get out before he can get me, please, oh please, let me get out."

She ran out of the front door and into the yard. The wind stirred the grass and dust and the coming rain was a gray sheet in the sky, but she didn't see it. She only ran. She knew he was coming and she ran. The water began to pelt the earth around her, sending little gray clouds of dust into the air around her feet. She looked over her shoulder behind her. He wasn't there. She stopped. She looked all around. She couldn't see him. Why didn't Momma come home? Maybe she'd believe her now.

The rain began to fall harder and harder. She couldn't go back to the house. That left one other place. She didn't want to go there, but the rain began to beat her and, not knowing what else to do, she ran to the barn.

It was dry there. It smelled of hay. She shook the water from her hair and looked back at the house. He was in there, she knew. He was waiting. But she wouldn't go back. She wouldn't, not in a million years. Not till Momma came home.

"Celie May."

She whirled as she heard a sort of sound come out of her mouth. It must have been her, she thought. Jess didn't sound like that. He was there, smiling, that look in his eyes. He started to walk toward her. She couldn't move. He held out his hand to touch her, but her feet backed away from him.

"Celie May," he said softly. "Celie May."

She turned and ran to the loft. He was walking toward her. There was no place to go but up.

"Jess," she said, climbing the steps of the ladder. "Don't. Please don't."

"I ain't gonna hurt you, Sugar," he said, his voice all concern. "Don't cry. I ain't gonna hurt you."

She hadn't known she was crying. She didn't stop but got to the top of the ladder and jumped onto the floor of the loft. He was climbing up now, telling her not to cry over and over again. She watched the muscles move under his shirt for a moment and felt the fear grip her tightly and squeeze. A bale of hay was close to the edge of the loft. She pushed it next to the ladder and off of the wooden boards with her arms. It struck Jess on the side of his head and on his shoulders, causing him to lose his balance. He hung in mid-air for an instant, his face looking up at her, before he fell.

It took a long time, she thought, before he hit the floor of the barn, before she heard the thud and the sharp cracking as something snapped somewhere. His mouth twisted and he groaned. She steadied herself on the edge of the loft amid the sweet-smelling hay, looking down at her brother. She didn't move. She only stared. The bullet sounds of the rain on the tin roof of the barn were what finally roused her.

"Celie May," Jess said. "Celie May."

She couldn't feel anything. She could hear and she could see, but she couldn't feel anything. She went quickly to the house and the telephone, dripping water all over the floor when she got inside. Momma had all sorts of questions, but Celie only told her to come home. Now. The doctor said he'd get out there as soon as he could. Celie was to get blankets and a pillow and make her brother as comfortable as possible. She set the receiver down slowly on its hook after she said good-bye to the doctor and looked at her hand, so calm, so strange, feeling like it didn't belong at the end of her arm.

She went to the hall closet where Momma kept extra bed things for company, got two blankets and a pillow, and pushing her hair out of her eyes, walked out of the house and into the rain, out to the barn which stood like an icon against the gray, ashen sky.

**A. Melody Faul:** I am a counselor at the Rape Crisis Center in my hometown of Lafayette, Louisiana. I have a Bachelor's and a Master's degree from the University of Southwestern Louisiana in English Liberal Arts and spend my time teaching, writing, and looking for diverse ways to pay the bills. My interest in the subject of this story began when a close friend confided in me that she had been incestuously assaulted by her brother. In my outrage, I decided that my friend's story and, as it turned out, the story of several other people I knew should be told in some way. My way became "Lessons."

# Rhubarb on 27th Street

I have always depended on
these strange
stalks' knowing
not to spill their poison
my knowing
where to break
off the deadly leaves
Faith makes good pies

Black men in the alley behind this secret
downtown rhubarb patch know
I'm just a good downhome girl behind my mind
doot de doot de doot walking along
with my brown bag full of fat red stems the men
signifying Unh, unh, gonna be some good pie
at your house tonight save me one little piece?
Grin sidestep doot de doot what happened

in the alley
when I was thirteen
(hard little peaches
in a white lace
blouse, thrill
of new hips)
the white boys'
poison spilled
on my thighs my lips

didn't mean a thing.  I see them on the street
and speak to them their faces break in the strangest
places they were my friends I never depended on them.

**Claudia Linde:** I teach writing at a university near Baltimore and am editor/director of a small publishing company. I also work with inmates at a medium-security prison for men, many of whom are convicted rapists. After the gang-attack that "celebrated" my pubescence, an attack by an "our gang" bunch of neighborhood boys not much older than myself, nothing seems to scare me very much: the worst is already over. A woman's spirit—like rhubarb—doesn't have to be completely poisoned just because of one poisonous part.

# The Hunt of the Gazelle

I stopped wearing shorts in summer
that man took freedom
breaking through my window seizing space,
male madness demanding.

Finding his face hunting the animal
vomit rising in throat
trapped—movement halted—
death in the rape state,
grasping parts
of the blue and white handwoven spread
scented by familiar safe memories
protecting nakedness
I lost the pure white soft young flesh
covering delicate boned graceful innocence
hearing my words, please no.

Bearing the agony of escapelessness
time endless
he tore away describing my body moving
in blood red jogging shorts
running from him
on early summer mornings.

**Ann Vosper:** I am a single woman living in Manhattan. I have an
M.Ed. in Child Study/Curriculum Development from Tufts University and an M.S. in Reading from the Bank Street College.

I wrote "The Hunt of the Gazelle" three years after the assault
occurred. No incident had affected my life so abruptly and intensely as that one. It was through this experience that I found the
meaning of turning my life over to God. In the days following the
occurrence, I also discovered the releasing of emotion through
writing.

# walking, motion memory exercise

I've spent so much of my life thinking about this, and so much time being angry at my father that I'm tired of it. I have spent my whole thinking cognitive life trying to protect my parents from this horrible thing, this secret. as if they weren't participants in what happened. when I was twenty-two I had my first consenting sexual experience with a man and suddenly was flooded with memories about sex between my father and me. I was overwhelmed. I tried to kill myself by injecting meat tenderizer into my veins. I became very depressed (no shit). these are all general feelings not very specific—lying in bed waiting for my father listening to the leaky toilet run between flushes across the hall (it gurgled when flushed). my grandmother is in town—hearing footsteps quietly a screen door sliding open then closed more footsteps shuffling now—stop—my door opened—close eyes. breathe shallow feign sleep—he is not fooled—there is a cricket in my room in the wall I think it stops chirping as the door opens the only sound is the toilet—my father sits on the edge of my bed he is quiet—just sitting there. the cricket resumes chirping—my father reaches under the sheets and touches me—my stomach/chest I am motionless holding my breath. a light goes on down the hall my father stiffens someone walks to the bathroom the light goes on someone pees the toilet is flushed it gurgles it is flushed again more gurgling the handle is moved rapidly it makes a clicking sound the water in the sink is on someone is washing their hands (I know it is not my brother he never washes his hands at night) the water is turned off—my father sighs—the light goes off in the bathroom—the sink is dripping—I look up there are seven light colored patches on the third black wooden beam which runs from the west to the east above my head—there are eleven beams in all—with two cross beams—termites I think—those light patches the cricket is real loud now—my father slides his hand lower on my body it is sticky with sweat from nervousness I tighten my stomach/my whole self—as the hand moves under my underwear. the sink is still dripping I try to regulate my breathing to the drips to my father's breathing—he removes my underwear I roll away from him he grabs me it's useless to struggle my underwear is caught on my foot I hold on to it tightly with my toes and try to slide it over my ankle with my other foot just a little farther success now at least I'm not naked I feel safer somehow my father whispers "relax I won't hurt you" I grab my pillow and hug it—my underwear have little ladybugs on them my father is excited now he is stiff he rolls/pushes me onto my back I close my eyes he elbows me in the thigh forcing my legs apart the pillow is over my head hiding me——pain the bed squeaks and he is mad—hurting me—thrust——

I am a mountain lion.
I am eight years old.
I live in the city.
Mountain lions
live in the mountains.
They live high up in the mountains
in dark caves
and no one bothers them
and they never come down from the mountains
to the people who live at the bottom
except once in a while
just to visit
sometimes they come down and watch
the people and sometimes
when they watch the people they stay out of the way
of the people but if the people attack them they kill the
    people.

Mountain lions are strong.
They have sharp teeth.
They have sharp claws.
When mountain lions come out of their caves
they go up in trees.
When someone comes by I jump
I pounce from my tree on my brother
I never kill my brother
I just like to scare him.

It does scare him then I make nice growls
to show him I'm not going to eat him.

When Daddy comes by I pounce on him
I roar and growl and
bite his leg.
I grab his leg and won't let go.
He pretends he is scared
and I pretend he is hurt.
He pretends to scream for help
and my mother comes from the kitchen
and brings a plate of cookies
and a bowl of milk.
She says "please let my husband go"
and I do and I eat
and I make nice growls
and they pet me.
If I were strong and a real mountain lion
I wouldn't let go of Daddy's leg
I would tear his leg to pieces
and then the rest of him and eat him
but I'm not that strong so I have to pretend
that milk and cookies are
pieces of Daddy
and I let them think
he has been saved
but he hasn't.
I always get him
again.

I never pounce
on my mother.
When she comes by my tree I jump
down and make nice
growls. Sometimes
she pets me. Sometimes
she tells me to stop
playing games so I crawl back
into my cave.

At home I am a mountain lion
all the time.
Even when I'm not acting
like a mountain lion I am
a mountain lion.
When I have to do something human
like get dressed
or go to the store
I am pretending to be human.

When anyone comes to visit I hide
in my cave.
If they're nice
I come out of my cave
and rub against their legs
and growl nice
and get in their lap
and curl up.

If they're not nice,
I stay in my cave and sneak out
when they're not looking
and run back to my mountain.
If they're really not nice
I stay in my cave
until they forget me then I crawl
out quietly
and pounce.

At school I am a mountain lion too.
I have to pretend to be human
most of the time except
at recess or when the teacher leaves the room
or when I'm in the bathroom
with the other kids.
At school I don't pounce
I scratch.
My teeth aren't very sharp
but my fingernails are long and sharp
and with my claws

I scratch the other kids
I scratch them hard
I make them bleed
I make them cry.


**Ellen:** I was molested until after age 21 when I chose to hurt someone myself. I was a bus driver and there was a little boy I identified with. I started to fantasize about him. I eventually did molest him. Watching him hurt and change from being trusting to fearful convinced me to seek help for both of us. Seeing him hurt validated much of my own hidden pain. The young man has gotten therapy and is doing fine. I have been in a psych hospital and am continuing treatment. I am living in an apartment now and working part time. I go to support groups. This experience changed me forever. I am able to love my family again, but I'm never again going to let anyone hurt me as much as they did.

# Rebirth of Life

This story about myself is very true. I never thought I would be able to live my life to its fullest. I was one of the blessed ones I think. My name is Barbara. I don't mind telling anyone about my life because I can live without feeling guilty for a change.

My mother's name is Alice. She really had a problem, she used to beat us for anything we did. She used to tie me to a chair and tie a diaper around my mouth to make me sit still and be quiet, so she could sleep. One time I was left babysitting my baby sister and brother, and they wouldn't be quiet, so I tied them to chairs and put diapers around their mouths. My aunt came over and saw them. She told my mother when she came home. My mother was mad as hell, so she took the shotgun and whipped me with the butt of it. Then she turned around and told me to put my head on the washer. I did and she came down with a meat cleaver. I moved my head just in time because she hit the washer and knocked the paint off it.

Another night before I started school, she was asking me some math problems and I gave her a wrong answer. She knocked me off the couch, then went to the kitchen and got an ironing cord and beat me. Where she hit me the cord just cut my skin, I was really bleeding bad. My aunt came over to visit, saw me and passed out.

My mother also beat me for killing the goldfish we had. She beat me with the ironing cord again, then threw me out in the front yard. A lady named Mrs. Horne who lived across the street picked me up and took me to her house and doctored on me. She went to talk to my mother who told her it was no concern of hers because she didn't have us.

My mother used to go out all the time, she never had time for us at all. She would leave us at home for 3 or 4 days with nothing to eat. Mrs. Horne would come over to check on us. Sometimes she would take us to this place called Ma Brown's to eat because we wouldn't have eaten for 2 days, sometimes 3. My mother would really trip out and call us little black sons of bitches, stupid asses and anything else she could think of. We used to ask Mrs. Horne not to tell mama anything because she would beat the hell out of us.

One night when she had gone out drinking, we were asleep when she came home. She came into our bedroom and started stabbing us for no reason at all. I was stabbed 13 times. After the first few stabs I could hear my meat pop. She didn't take us to the doctor at all. She made us get up and change the bloody sheets, then we slept on the hide-a-bed in the living room just bleeding. The next morning she up and doctored on us and told us to tell people we fell in some glass. I told that lie for about 10 years. I hated her for what she did, but I loved her too. I really didn't think everyone had to live that way.

I was nine at the time my stepfather molested me. Being so scared of my mother didn't help at all. I figured she would never believe me. Anyway she was always too busy to have a talk with us about anything. I don't know how I put up with the pain unless I was just to scared to say no. My stepfather did that for years, and he used to pay me to keep my mouth closed, to not tell my mother. He would even take me out in the car and do the same thing all over again.

My mother became a nurse at the age of 35. I hated for her to work at night because he would come into my bedroom and wake me up. Sometimes I would play sleep hoping he would leave me alone, but he never did. He'd pick me up and take me to their bedroom and start fingering me. Then he would start saying suck my tit, that feels good and suck my prick. I felt bad about it for years.

Then my stepfather's brother raped me at the age of 12. That's a night I will always remember. He came into our bedroom. I slept on the bottom bunk. Everyone was at home, so at first I thought I was dreaming, but it was true. When I got up the next morning and looked at my bed and gown, they were really bloody. I was scared stiff, I didn't get up, I jumped back in bed until everyone else left the back part of the house. Then I threw the sheets in the trash can in the alley. I have lived a scared life.

I used to go on these rampages. I never knew why I would get mad and just tear up stuff and all this mess would go through my head, then I would want to kill myself. I was tired of coping with it and life. After I was married in 1970, I used to try and tell my husband what had happened. He would tell me I brought it upon myself, so I felt that way until last year.

I went to a counseling center for depression and to find out

31

what made me go into a rage every so often. I finally figured it out. What had happened to me had stayed inside me. I wouldn't let it or the hate and mixed feelings about it come out.

I always loved my mother. I tried to reach out to her, but she wouldn't accept it. This year I told her all about it. She tried to put the blame back on me, but I told her I lived with it for years and it wasn't my fault at all. It was hers because she would never listen. After a year of therapy I feel great about myself. I feel proud because I have four kids, and I have always raised them different from the way I was raised.

My therapist told me she never knew why I didn't get as bad as my mother. But I lived that life and I know just what it can do to you. I don't want any of my kids to go through life the way I did.

**Barbara Sanders:** The problems I had to go through in life have helped me to deal with my four children. I now have a government job working with people and I love it. I didn't feel strong and I never knew I could control my life so well until I really had to make a stand on my own. But you have to work at life in order to be what you want to be, so don't give up.

# The Dawning

It wasn't the same this time. It hurt more. The headache which usually started above her left temple and worked its way across the top of her head, to the lump of bone behind her right ear, was concentrated across the front of her head. The slightest movement of her head or body caused a throbbing increase in the pain as well as the sensation of green and yellow lights behind her closed eyelids. She tried very hard not to move. The dried tears left sticky tracks on her swollen cheek. She held the tatters of a rag doll clutched in her frail arms. Light from the overhead fixture in the hallway flowed constantly through the space beneath the door. Christy watched the light intenty.

The world outside the window of her room began to change from black to green to rosy and finally to the normalcy of morning. As the light through the window increased, Christy shifted her gaze to it. Gradually, she began to relax her hold on the doll. The pain in her head subsided enough to allow her to move. She began to take inventory of herself. She rearranged the torn nightdress over her scratched legs. The blood on her thighs had dried a dark brown. As she stretched her body out under the heavy patchwork quilt she let out an unintentional whimper. The muscles on the inside of her thighs protested.

As the morning grew, Christy began to slide into sleep. Almost before she could drop off, it seemed, her mother was shaking her shoulder. "Get up Christy. It's time to go to school. You can't sleep all day. Hurry up."

Christy clutched the worn quilt under her chin to keep the warmth in. Her mother stood over the bed, casting her shadow on Christy's face, her arms folded in characteristic impatience under her full breasts. She turned to leave the room. Sunlight framed the worn pink fabric of the robe, which covered her lean haunches. A faint barn smell still hung in the room.

"Hurry up and get through in the bathroom. Your father is going to want in there pretty soon, and you don't want to get in his way. You wouldn't want a whipping would you?" Her mother left the room.

Christy threw off the warm quilt and slid out of the bed. She made a shivering dash out of the unheated room, across the narrow hall into the warm cozy bathroom. She bathed quickly, not taking the time to run water into the bathtub. The warm water would feel good on her sore body. She wrapped a towel around her slight body and ran, still shivering, back to her bedroom, her ruined nightdress clutched in a useless ball. She dressed as quickly as her sore body would permit. She put on warm socks and jeans to protect her against the cold winter day. The denim chaffed at her tender legs.

The Cap'n Crunch and a half-gallon milk container were sitting on the kitchen table. Her mother sat at one end of the table reading the newspaper and sipping carefully on a steaming cup of coffee.

"Eat your cereal. The bus will be here soon."

Christy heard the bathroom door close with a bang. Moments later a rush of water cascaded through the drain in the kitchen wall, and the water pipes rattled. She ate her cold cereal hurriedly. When the flow of water ceased, her mother put down her paper and got up and walked to the three-burner stove. She took a match from the container on the kitchen wall and scratched it across the iron surface of the stove. She lit the front burner on the stove and placed a heavy skillet on it. She arranged six slices of bacon in the skillet. She took a bowl of eggs out of the icebox and sat them on the counter next to the stove.

The sound of heavy boots descending the stairs made Christy eat her cereal faster. Her father entered the room with the noise and confidence which he carried with him always. Her mother, who had poured him a cup of coffee as soon as she heard him on the stairs, began to crack eggs into the skillet from which she had removed the bacon. The warm animal smell and good-humored vitality of her father brought the room to life. As he passed behind Christy's chair, he reached down and ruffled her hair. She colored slightly. Her hand darted hastily to her hair to put it back in order.

"Good morning, Christy."

"Good morning, Daddy." She bent over her cereal bowl not eating. Christy pushed her chair back from the table and started to get up.

"Don't leave yet. I like to talk to you."

34

"I have to catch the school bus." She felt the weight of the cereal in her stomach and the rough denim rubbing on her raw legs.

"Hell, you don't need to go to school. You're smart enough already. If you stayed home, you could help me with the chores."

"No. I have to catch the school bus." Christy pushed the nearly empty cereal bowl away from her.

Christy's mother put a steaming plate of bacon and eggs in front of the father. She patted her tightly bound hair as if to insure that it was still in place. She finished packing the lunch pail which Christy carried to school and set it on the table in front of the girl. "Hurry up Christy, or you'll miss your bus."

Christy got up from the table and started for her coat. Her father reached out with his strong hairy arm and encircled her waist. "Give your old man a kiss before you go kiddo." He pulled her to him roughly, tightening his hold on her waist. Christy bent her head to his and gave him a hesitant kiss on the cheek. With one last squeeze and a pat on the butt, Christy's father released her and turned to eating his breakfast. Her mother sat silently, looking at her coffee cup.

Christy struggled into her warm flannel coat. Clutching her school books in one arm, she grabbed her lunch pail and fumbled with the kitchen door. Finally getting the door open, she hurried out of the house. The sun, which had promised warmth earlier in the morning, was now concealed behind a growing bank of dark grey clouds. She walked briskly past the frozen hog pens and the towering barn and down the twisting lane toward the road. When she was out of sight of the house, she stopped. She looked back at the house. All she could see of it was the smoke curling out of the chimney. It floated aimlessly in the still morning air. Tears began to form in her eyes. She stood there for a moment, looking at the smoke. Then she heard the horn of the school bus at the end of the lane. Panicking, she turned and began to run. She broke off of the path and through a patch of brambles for a more direct route to the bus. The branches lashed against her legs as she ran.

Christy came into sight of the bus just as Mrs. Chalmers was about to drive off. She ran, panting, to the bus, climbed the steep steps, and gazed into the bright smiling face of the bus driver.

"Good morning Christy. I was afraid you were sick again." Mrs. Chalmers put the bus in gear and carefully eased out the clutch.

"No, Ma'am. I'm sorry I made you wait." Christy clung to the vertical bar behind the driver's seat, still looking at the soft profile.

"You'd better go sit down now, honey. It's safer."

"Yes Ma'am. Mrs. Chalmers, can I come eat lunch with you again today?"

"Sure, Honey, but you go sit down now."

"Yes Ma'am." Christy smiled as she worked her way back to the nearest empty seat. She sat watching the driver and smiling as the bus moved down the country road.


**Michael Sellers:** The experience related in "The Dawning" is that of someone very close to me. In an effort to help that person deal with the situation and to eventually dispel the feelings of guilt which a victim often feels, I have applied whatever skill I have to showing the point of view of the victim.

## Untitled

some big occasion
this big dinner
at Auntie's
three phone books
and me
piled high on the chair
Uncle Bill
pushes me in
hands that linger
around my hips
purse my lips
and ask for more
this and that
all this attention
for me
some big occasion
this big dinner
some retire to relax
we to play
down the stairs we tumble
I fear
what?
behind the pool table
behind the tool cabinet
behind the refrigerator
filled with cream soda
I stand shivering
naked
eyes closed
feeling your grin
stained
hot on my face

your wet kisses
Uncle Bill
with hands that linger
to this day
even


**Diane R. Bramble:** Three years ago I moved to Boulder, Colorado, and 2,000 miles away from the place of my incest. My deliberate attempt to run away only drew me closer to my experience. Memories catalyzed my accelerated process as feelings of isolation, fear, depression, suicide, anger, sadness, and sorrow all surfaced and pointed me in the direction of change.

I began a ritualistic, painful search to find my anger and redirect it towards the much deserved source. With the caring guidance of my therapist, Molly Gierasch, and my loving friends, I rediscovered words as an empowering means of purging and healing.

# Want Some Candy, Little Girl?

Want some candy, little girl?
If you sit with me a while,
    I'll let you have some.
What kind of candy?
It's round and soft, and white sugar comes
    out when you lick it.
Do you want some?
It's ok if you've never had that kind of
    candy before, I'll teach you.
Put your mouth on me, go ahead, don't
    be afraid.
Wait, why are you stopping?
This candy gets angry when you don't pay
    attention to it.
That's it! Press a little harder now,
    and try not to choke.
When you feel the sugar in your mouth,
    swallow,
And say, yum.


**Lisa A. Lahaie:** Writing and publishing this poem have been important steps in my healing process. Many years elapsed before I could even accept my own abuse. The main instigator of my healing, however, has been the love I've found in Jesus Christ. In the midst of pain, anger, guilt, and shame, the Lord offered His special brand of help. In Him I've found a release for all the emotions I felt. In His infinite wisdom, Jesus saw the abused child and felt compassion for her. His love poured through as He picked the child up into His arms and carried her away.

# What Was It Like, How Does It Feel?

She was the child in white cotton panties.
He was the kind man.

She was the mouth.

This is a true story. A child's story.
She was the good little girl.

He was the tongue.

For years. In, in, in. The same story.
The family's favorite friend.

She didn't tell.

Now her hands are fists. He is the pillow.
Out. Out. Out. This is her bed.

And stay dead.

**Martha Collins:** I teach creative writing at the University of Massachusetts—Boston, where I've directed the Creative Writing Program for a number of years. I've published a book of poems, *The Catastrophe of Rainbows* (Cleveland State, 1985), and edited a collection of essays on the poet Louise Bogan; I've also published poems in numerous periodicals and anthologies. I've just completed my first novel.

# Good-by Dick. Good-by Jane.
# Good-by Funny, Funny Baby.

## I

By the time they had gotten off the trolley and walked across the street to the Bridgeport train station, Milly had worked herself into a state that could only be described as hysterical. Now, waiting on the platform in the full afternoon heat of a very humid day for the train that would carry the little girl beside her down to Greenwich, her voice was racing high and breathless and shivery

"Now. Now, Elizabeth. Mind your manners. Mind your manners. Scrub your nails before you come to the dinner table and, and, oh! don't forget to unfold your napkin and spread it in your lap. And, and, oh, yes! there are seven clean hankies in your suitcase, and, and, oh! remember to wear your shower cap when you bathe so your curls will hold and . . ."

The little girl stood stiffly, staring intently down the tracks that shimmered in the heat. She wore a white organdy dress, white socks, white patent leather shoes and a big white bow affixed to one of the 56 dark, corkscrew ringlets that had been wound to her scalp, pulled white and tight, the night before. She had never been on a train before.

". . . and don't scratch, and, oh, Elizabeth," she said, touching the child's shoulder, "if they should ask, say that I'm head buyer at Malleys. Don't tell them that I'm still working the cosmetic counter. It's simpler that way." At this Milly's smile was half conspiratorial, half pleading. The little girl nodded, then returned her attention to the tracks where the train, looking small as a toy, was just rounding the far off bend.

"And, oh! if they should give you any presents, say 'Oh, it's so-oo beautiful! Oh! Thank you!'" Saying this Milly clasped her small nervous hands together just under her heart-shaped little face, and, cocking her head to one side, looked upward, her fine, round eyebrows arched above wide, childlike eyes. Elizabeth watched this illustration with a mixture of sincere admiration and some-

41

thing else that made her feel uncomfortable. She thought her mother was very, very pretty. She was so slender and frail and delicate and sweet as the lily-of-the-valley scent that she always wore. But, suddenly, despite her brand new dress with eyelets and her 56 ringlets and her patent leather shoes, Elizabeth felt, standing next to Milly, terribly big and hopelessly clumsy. Suddenly she didn't want to go to spend the week with Cousin Clara and her husband Howard Worthington, Ph.D. She was sure she wouldn't be able to pull it off. "Mother?" she began.

The train bore down on the two, grinding and hissing and giving off a terrible, inhuman heat.

"Oh! Oh my goodness!" Milly said, bending down to give one of the child's curls an extra and totally redundant twist. A black porter swung down to the platform. Milly handed him the ticket. "She's to get off at Greenwich," she said in a soft voice, breathless still, but lower now. "Spending a week with my cousin and her husband," this casually, almost carelessly. "Would you be so kind as to see that she doesn't miss her stop?" Her smile was sweet, her eyes wide.

"Yes, ma'm," the porter said, taking the small suitcase and shopping bag from Milly's hand and putting them on the platform between the cars. "Come along, little lady," he said, extending his hand to the child.

"Go ahead, darling," Milly said, stepping back. "This good man will tell you when you're there."

Elizabeth placed her hand in the porter's whose huge palm felt surprisingly smooth and soft, and felt herself being pulled gently up onto the steps of the train. But suddenly Milly stepped forward again and grasped her other hand so that for a moment she was stretched, arms extended, between the two. Squeezing her hand tightly, Milly whispered in her ear "Show them, baby. Show them that despite everything, I've brought you up to be a perfect little lady." Then she let go and stepped back again. Her thin lips were drawn into a brave little smile, but her eyes were misty.

Elizabeth felt a terrible pang of anxiety clutch at her stomach. Her mother looked so small and forlorn standing down on the platform all by herself.

"She'll be all right," the porter said in a soft, deep voice. Startled, Elizabeth looked up at him, sure that he had looked down on her head and picked out her thoughts. But his reassuring smile was for Milly, who nodded bravely and gave a spritely little wave. "Now let's find you a nice seat by the window, miss," he said to Elizabeth. He pushed the door which opened with a long sigh, and Elizabeth preceded him into the train. But Milly was there again, her spiked heels clicking on the metal platform behind them. "Just one more thing. One more thing," she said apologetically, laying her hand lightly on the porter's back. Elizabeth thought she heard another long sigh and looked up quickly, but the porter was nodding and standing aside, a smile fixed on his lips.

With a furtive glance into the train, Milly pulled the little girl aside and, bending down, hissed into her ear, "Don't talk to any strangers." She pulled away and nodded solemnly, locking eyes with Elizabeth in a very serious way. "Remember," she said, her index finger raised in warning.

## II

There were nothing but strangers on the train. Elizabeth sat by herself next to the window, careful not to lay her arm on the grimy sill. In the seat in front of her sat a stout woman with an enormous bosom. The feathers on her hat quivered incessantly with the motion of the train. Diagonally across the aisle a girl in a tall hat with a wide brim and a lacy black veil crossed and recrossed her legs, each time tugging at the pencil slim skirt of her man-tailored suit, and refused to talk to the young sailor in the seat behind her who every now and then leaned forward and addressed her over the back of the seat. Elizabeth thought it was very unpatriotic of the girl to ignore the sailor who was, after all, one of "our boys" and might still get killed in the war. After all, even if the dirty Nazis had already been beaten, there were still the dirty Japs to contend with.

The girl wore very high heeled open shoes with a slender strap around the ankle. Her toe nails were painted bright red. Milly said that girls who painted their toenails were not at all refined. The young sailor, on the other hand, looked very refined and clean cut in his spanking white uniform. Elizabeth was studying his profile when he looked across the aisle and caught her. She was about to look away quickly when he said "Hi, toots!" and winked at her. His eyes were very blue and twinkly, his grin big and boyish. Elizabeth regarded him solemnly for a moment, trying to decide. Then she winked back. The sailor laughed, tossing his head back, and then turned his attention to the girl's arched foot in her high open shoe that was now swinging out into the aisle and back, out into the aisle and back.

Elizabeth was enchanted. She stared at the sailor, trying to take in all his features at once and commit them to memory because from now on that would be exactly how she would describe her father. Milly had told her when she'd started school last year that if anyone should ask, she could say that her daddy was killed in the war. "It's simpler that way," Milly had said. Elizabeth didn't mind telling people that her daddy had been killed in the war. Sometimes she didn't even wait to be asked but volunteered the information in a small voice. She liked the way people, even other children, would say "Oh." Sometimes it brought a lump to her throat and tears to her eyes, the way they said "Oh," so sympathetically. In fact, she so much enjoyed the story of her daddy's untimely demise that sometimes she added embellishments of her own. "He never even got to see me," she'd say. "Never even knew if I was a boy or a girl." It made so much more of an appealing story than the truth that was her and Milly's family secret. Now, next time someone asked she would say "I only saw him once, but I remember him clear as day. He had the most twinkling blue eyes and he always called me Toots."

The sailor looked across the aisle, apparently having felt her staring at him, and before she could stop herself, Elizabeth smiled at him.

"Kind of little, ain't you, toots," he said, "to be taking a train ride all by yourself?"

Elizabeth looked away quickly. "Ain't"! "Ain't"! The children in the neighborhood that she and Milly were forced to live in, temporarily, said "ain't." She was not allowed to play with the children in the neighborhood because they came from Irish or Italian families and were not refined at all. Her disappointment was so acute that for a moment she had to fight back tears. When she had herself under control, she fumbled through the shopping bag at her feet and, carefully keeping her eyes to herself, pulled out a book. *Fun with Dick and Jane*. Although she could read practically anything that was put before her, this book was by far her favorite and she had been overjoyed when, at the end of first grade, her teacher had let her take it home, to keep. The pages were worn from the many times she had turned them. Now she looked at Mother

44

in her apron. She looked at Dick and Jane and funny, funny baby. She looked at Spot and fluffy little Puff. They were playing on the broad front lawn of the big white house with green shutters. And, look, look, look. Here comes Father. Father wears a suit and a necktie. Father carries a briefcase. See Dick run. See Jane run. See funny, funny baby run. They are running to meet Father. They are happy, happy, happy. They are happy because Father is home. Mother, standing in the doorway wiping her hands on her pretty apron, is happy, even though she does not run—ever. Happy, happy Dick. Happy, happy Jane. Funny, funny baby.

## III

There was no "little lady" this time. There was no deep, soft voice. There wasn't even a long sigh, hidden. There was just, "OK. You get off at the next stop. Come on," and a suitcase brought down from the high rack and plunked on the seat beside her. Elizabeth picked up the shopping bag and the small suitcase and tugged them clumsily into the aisle. The sailor, who had slumped in his seat, stirred and for a moment seemed about to get up to help her, but she struggled past him, her head held high and, she hoped, haughtily. But her haughtiness disappeared as she stood on the wobbling platform in between the cars and waited for the train to stop. She knew that somewhere far ahead someone had reached out a very ordinary human hand and pulled a brake. But she felt . . . What she felt was the churning, roaring, straining momentum of the great machine. And she was afraid. It's too late, she thought. They'll never be able to stop it now. She felt that the brutal, hurtling energy that carried her forward must surely be far beyond the control of any human hand. They would never be able to stop it now. Never. And then what would become of her?

The train did, however, eventually grate to a stop. Elizabeth was flung like a rag doll, first against the porter's indifferent back, then backward into the corseted body of the woman with the trembling feathers in her hat whose breath exploded—woof!

The porter swung down onto the platform. He extended his hand to the child, but his eyes, smiling now, were riveted on the couple to whom he handed her belongings. "I guess you're here to meet the little lady," he said in a soft, deep voice. But their eyes were riveted on Elizabeth who remained uncertainly on the steps, the woman's taking in the child with a hungry sort of intensity, the man's appraising, critical, narrowed slightly as if he were squinting into the sun. But he wasn't because the sun, low in the sky now, was behind him, sprawling his long, flat shadow at his feet. His arms were folded across his chest and his chin was pulled in tight. He looked as if he were deliberating on a proposition. Finally he nodded to the porter who picked the girl up under her arms and set her down at his feet. The man dropped some money into the porter's soft, smooth, expectant palm.

## IV

The street was broad and elm-arched. The front lawns were wide and trimmed along the sidewalks. Elizabeth sat on the front step of the big white house with green shutters, stroking the little orange kitten that curled in her lap. On the grass sat the old fashioned wicker doll carriage that Cousin Clara had brought down from the attic. In the carriage was an old fashioned baby doll. Cousin Clara had made some new clothes for the doll. She had made the sunsuit that Elizabeth wore. Now Cousin Clara was in the kitchen making dinner. She was wearing an apron. And Elizabeth was waiting, looking down the sun-spotted sidewalk, stroking the little orange kitten that curled in her lap. Cousin Howard had given her the little orange kitten, not to take home, but to play with when she visited. She spotted him when he crossed the street a full block away. "Wait here, pussy," she said, and darted down the sidewalk.

Cousin Howard stopped and put his briefcase down on the sidewalk, stooped down and held his arms wide. Elizabeth ran. She ran and ran and ran. Cousin Howard swept his arm between her legs, and, clutching her buttocks, swung her high into the air. As usual, she gasped and giggled. As usual, she grasped for his head.

"Have you been a good girl today?" Cousin Howard said sternly, putting her down again. Elizabeth nodded, beaming up at him. "Then up you go!" he said, lifting her to his shoulders. "Giddyup!" Elizabeth commanded. "Giddyup!" Howard trotted down the sidewalk. He wore a suit and a necktie. Elizabeth giggled and giggled and held on tightly to his head. She was happy, happy, happy. This was her favorite time of day.

But there were other times, too. There were the early mornings

46

when she sat perched on the cold rim of the bathtub and watched Cousin Howard shave. He would glance at her sidelong in the mirror in a special sort of way that made her feel shivery, and when he was finished, he would rub his cheek against hers saying "How's that? Close enough?" Then Cousin Clara would serve them breakfast on the breezeway.

And there was bedtime. She would be bathed and brushed and in the pretty nightgown that Cousin Howard had brought home for her one evening. "Well, model it. Model it," he'd said and watched her through narrowed eyes while she pirouetted around, holding one arm above her head, at which he'd laughed heartily, while Cousin Clara smiled that strange smile that bothered Elizabeth because it made her face look sad instead of happy. She would place a light, quick kiss in the hollow of Clara's cheek and then Howard would take her upstairs. There, in the guest room with the pink flowered wall paper and the lacy white curtains, he would hold her in his lap and read to her. Elizabeth would listen very carefully because every time he finished a story he would quiz her. "What," he'd say, "do bears do in the wintertime?" "Where is the longest river in the world?" "What is the capital of Connecticut?" If she could answer correctly, he'd say, "Um hum," or "Yes. Of course." But if she couldn't! Then he'd say, "Come, now, Elizabeth! A six-year-old who doesn't know that!" or "Really, I just read that to you. How could you forget so soon?" Her failure reduced her to a state of panic and despair. Hadn't she overheard Howard saying to Clara, "She seems quite bright." And then in a tone unmistakably derisive, "It's hard to believe she's Milly's child." This chance comment posed quite a problem for Elizabeth, who had never before troubled herself over whether she might be bright or not. And, of course, she had just assumed that Milly was smart. But then, hadn't Milly herself said that Cousin Clara's husband was a genius. A Harvard Graduate. Elizabeth hadn't known exactly what a Harvard Graduate meant, but Milly's tone of deep respect left no doubt that it was something to be impressed about. Then, too, Milly said that the reason Cousin Howard was not in the war was because his job was Vital to the National Defense. Cousin Howard certainly was Somebody. So she listened harder and harder when he read to her, even though pleasing him with correct answers did give her some uncomfortable feelings, as if she were somehow being a traitor to her mother.

There were other times when she felt uncomfortable. For instance:

Cousin Howard had a habit of coming into her room in the middle of the night. The first time she had become aware of his presence, some movement next to the bed had awakened her with a start. There Cousin Howard stood. She had tried guiltily to fix her eyes on his face, but as he stood there so long and silently, they traveled down his body, pale in the moonlight that glanced through the dormer windows, across his flat stomach, down to where his private parts hung like a shadow between his legs. Her eyes had gone quickly back to his face, but then down again, following his eyes, drawing hers down, down. Then he had turned and without a word, left the room.

The next morning she'd thought that she'd dreamed it.

But the next night he came again. And the next and the next. And now sometimes he pulled the chair next to the bed and sat down. And now, sometimes, he took her hand and placed it between his legs where it was filled with parts limp and floppy as an earlobe.

In the daytime Elizabeth tried to put all this together with being a genius and a Harvard Graduate. She tried to put it together with being Vital to the National Defense and with the obvious fact that Milly considered Cousin Howard to have been a real "catch" for Clara. ("Clara was attractive, in a tall, statuesque sort of way, but there were those who thought I was the prettier one," Milly would say. "'If Clara has the bearing', they'd say, 'Milly has the profile.'" At this, Milly would always cock her head to one side and present to Elizabeth the profile that some people thought was prettier than Cousin Clara's "bearing.")

But none of this went together with Howard's strange nocturnal visits. The only thing that Elizabeth thought did go together with these visits was what Milly referred to as "Clara's tragedy." "When I came home with you, after my 'mistake'," as Milly always bitterly referred to her brief marriage to Elizabeth's father, "Clara said to me 'She's such a beautiful baby. You're so lucky, Milly.' Imagine! Clara with her wonderful marriage and beautiful home thinking that I was lucky! I think it absolutely broke her heart that she couldn't have a baby of her own, poor dear. It's been a real tragedy for her."

That piece of information did seem to go together with Cousin

Howard's visits. And Elizabeth felt, with a terrible mixture of pride and exhilaration and pity and guilt, that where Cousin Clara, whose large, blue-veined hands reached out so tentatively, almost shyly, had somehow failed, she, Elizabeth was somehow succeeding.

This notion made days alone with Clara long and uncomfortable—hoping that she didn't know, wondering what she'd do if she did know, wishing that she would not stare at her with those hungry eyes and that sad smile while Elizabeth hid in her heart the guilty little dream that began "When I'm grown up and Cousin Clara is dead. . ."

But there were other times, when they took her for walks down the sun-spotted sidewalk, one on either side, holding her hands, and the neighbors would pause in their gardening and smile and oh! it was better than *Fun with Dick and Jane* because there was only Elizabeth and she would pretend Mommy and pretend Daddy and pretend that the guest room in the big white house with green shutters was her own until another guilty little dream would form and suddenly she would ask to call Milly long distance and her heart would pound as the phone rang and rang and she'd go limp with relief when Milly's sweet, high voice would finally answer. "I miss you, mother." "I miss you, too. Show them, baby. Show them."

On the Sunday before she was to leave, Howard and Clara took her to the Bronx Zoo where she got to ride on a camel and watch the panda splashing in his pool and saw a strange, shy creature called a duck-billed platypus.

That night she was awake when Howard came silently to her room. He pulled the chair next to her bed and placed her hand between his legs but tonight, magically, there was something hard and long in the midst of the soft, limp parts. Howard closed his hand over her own, closing her fingers around the firm, capped shaft. He guided her hand up and down, up and down. The sound of his breathing filled the room. Filled the room with a terrible, unbearable expectancy. Something, Elizabeth knew, her eyes wide and straining into the darkness, something was going to happen. And whatever that something was, nothing, nothing could stop it now. Then. . .

She jerked away and leaped to the far side of the bed. Crouched there she stared horrified toward the shape that was

Howard who was slumped over, laughing very softly. Then "I'll be right back," he whispered.

The room was filled with an ear-ringing silence. Elizabeth held her hand, fingers spread wide, far away from her body. She thought that she might scream into the ear-ringing silence.

Howard returned carrying a wet wash cloth.

"Come here," he whispered hoarsely, but Elizabeth shook her head "no." "Elizabeth!" he hissed, reaching out for her. "Get over here!" She shrank back. He grabbed her, his fingers closing roughly around her upper arm, and jerked her across the bed. "Now stop your nonsense!" he said, shaking her slightly. "Stop it right now!" He was whispering, but it was as if he were shouting at her.

"Now," he said tightly. "Give me your hand. It's dirty."

He washed her hand and her arm with the wash cloth, then told her to go back to sleep. "Everything's all right," he said.

But she couldn't go back to sleep. She was wide awake now. And everything wasn't all right. It wasn't all right at all. He had wet her! And Elizabeth *knew* that *that* wasn't a nice thing to do. That wasn't a nice thing for *anyone* to do.

The next morning she did not watch Howard shave, but stayed in bed until she heard the big front door close behind him. Then, feeling a sudden pang of loss, she sprang to the window. Howard was going down the front walk. He was wearing a suit and a necktie. He swung his briefcase by his side. He . . .

Elizabeth went downstairs.

"Cousin Howard said to let you sleep, but he said to be a good girl on the train and he gave me a big kiss for you," Cousin Clara said. She lay her large hands lightly on Elizabeth's shoulders. Her big face, smiling sadly, came closer and closer. Elizabeth stiffened. Then drew away. She couldn't help it.

Tears sprang to Cousin Clara's eyes. She looked as if someone had smacked her sharply on the cheek.

"I'm sorry," Elizabeth wanted to say. "I'm sorry." But she couldn't.

At the train station Cousin Clara asked shyly if Elizabeth would like to come and stay with her and Cousin Howard again sometime soon. Elizabeth nodded "yes." It was simpler that way.

Another invitation did arrive very soon. Milly tore open the small, flowered envelope and read it aloud. "But, oh!" she said. "How can I send you now, after what you've done to your hair?"

Elizabeth looked up from the comic book that her new friend Theresa Gagliardi had loaned her. Her hair stood out all over her head, straight and bristly as a shaving brush, the root ends of the 56 curls that she had one by one cut off with Millie's manicure scissors.

"It doesn't matter," she said. "I don't want to go anyway."

"Why?" Milly said in the same stricken tone as when she'd first seen the hair.

"It's no fun there," Elizabeth said, forcing the words out over her secret knowledge. "Besides," she added, making herself look straight into her mother's puzzled, hurt, bewildered eyes, "I'm kind of little, ain't I, to take a train ride all by myself?"

**Evelyn Orr:** *All* things work for good. The hurt and angry little girl in this story is now the happiest person I know. She is me and I am she and we are one, whole and complete.

# Famous Monsters

Standing in the toy
aisle of K-Marts, a boy
who loves monsters, me,
fourteen, with a buck-twenty
stuffed in my pocket for
being a good kid or
mowing my grandpa's lawn,
leaving part of it undone
so I could get here in time
before they're all gone,
loving even the cellophane
wrapped around the boxes
full of Frankenstein
and Dracula pieces—
the absolute rage
of *Famous Monsters'*
inside back page.

It's so hard to choose.
The Hunchback of Notre Dame?
The Creature from the Black Lagoon?
I've got plenty of green paint
and two tubes of Testor's airplane
glue at home and . . .
                    Jeezus!
Will you look at that?

Some big guy in tennis shoes
coming this way, his fat
ass shoe-horned into some lame
pair of faded jeans,
number 76 in peeling
yellow on his blue jersey
pulled over his gut like a T-
shirted weather balloon,

bobbling nearer and nearer
until I could faint
from the smell
just like hell
and fish and chili beans.

And his eyes are like *feeling*
me, which ain't right at all,
so I . . . I act kind of casual,
pulling down a Wolfman,
looking at the price, shaking
my head and walking away.
He does the same, but it's faking
so he can follow me.

Walking down other aisles,
zig-zagging every
which way
I can,
I can't shake
this guy from my tail;
past manikins
and blue light sales,
the slapping noise
of cow-man's sneakers
follows me,
past shirts
and skirts
on hangers, in plastic, in piles,
men's wear and underwear
and dinnerware
and nowhere
to go, past
ladies' lingerie,
back-to-school for girls-n-boys,
past pets and parrots
and kids with their parents
smudging the glass to point
out a turtle, paddling through
an inch of water over slimy

stones and orange gravel, past
paper and glue
and notebooks and pipe joints,
wicker baskets, philodendrons,
bags of cowshit, reproductions
in gilt frames and—
                    how'd he
choose me?
Why
can't I
lose him?—
              safety in numbers;
these people are so dumb!

"Get out of my way!
Can't you see
Buffalo Bill
following me?"

Then, at last:
The Dressing Room . . .

Zip in, slide the curtain,
just keep still,
nothing's for certain,
pull up your feet
against your chest,
breathe quiet in your seat
as the old men undress.

Where are you now?
Where have you gone?
What have you done
that'll turn out wrong?

Nothing, nothing . . .
just sweat and the sound
of old men and teens
shuffling out, shuffling
in, to new suits, old jeans.

Nothing, nothing . . .
just the sound
of someone penning
a dirty poem
and the single sound
of
     a curtain
                    opening.

Howdy, cow-man . . .
Howdy, pard'ner.

He pushes my face into the mirror
so all I can see
is me and me,
so hard I think
it all might break,
and he still stinks
and my back aches
where he's pinning me
'tween the wing bones
with just one hand
while the other fumbles to unzip.
I pivot a hip
to look around
and his cock's as
big as a billy club, and harder.

His pants are on the ground
and he trips a bit
trying to nail me,
so I spin and lift a knee
up and he
buckles,
unbuckled,
and thoroughly fucked.

I want to step on his head
to let out the fat and
the air, brains and shit,

but I run, instead,
out of the Changing Room,
out of the store,
I run, across
no crossing
zones.
I run.

I keep on running.


**David Sosnowski:** I am a former editor of *permafrost*, the longest-running literary journal in Alaska. I have taught for the University of Alaska-Fairbanks and Madonna College and am currently teaching for the University of Detroit, Wayne State University and the University of Michigan-Dearborn. I have written for publications such as *Heartland*, *Metropolitan Detroit*, *Observer's Sky*, *Creative Computing*, *Alaska Today*, *Alaska Quarterly Review*, *Arizona English Bulletin*, *AWP Newsletter* and *Confrontations* and am learning how to stop hating myself and others.

*Famous Monsters* is the name of a monster fan magazine popular during the sixties and early seventies.

# Do You Want to Know What a
# Child Molester Looks Like?

When I was living in the Children's Home, the teenage girls there had a game where they would gang up on one girl and tear her clothes off. They trapped me in a room. I was terrified and tried to get to the door, but the way was blocked by all their snatching, clawing hands. I started screaming and begged them to stop, but they were too busy laughing and having a good time to pay attention.

If I were to go to those women now and tell them that they molested me, that they used my body for their momentary pleasure, and that I pay for their thoughtlessness with fear and distrust of others—they would be shocked. They would say—but there was no sex involved, no malice. We were just having a good time. Yet molest is not sex. Molest is the misuse of power. Molest is using a child's body for selfish needs. Molest is the betrayal of trust.

Do you want to know what a child molester looks like? Look in any mirror. Look at your family, your friends, your neighbors. Any human being is capable of any human action. And it is easy to ignore the needs of the powerless. It is easy to tell yourself you are doing them no harm because they do not have the power or the knowledge it takes to argue with you. If you resent the implications of these statements, your disbelief that you or someone you know could be harming a child allows the harm to continue.

Who's to say what harm is done? It is for the children to say, many years after the fact. The children who have grown up and can trace the harm in their lives like veins in their arms—here are the years of misery. Here are the years of pain and self-hate. Here is the job I didn't try for because I felt useless. Here are the times I allowed myself to be degraded because I felt worthless. Here are the loves I have lost because I felt cheap and used whenever I was touched.

Look at the children around you. Are they forced to pay for gifts with kisses and hugs they do not wish to give? Presents are supposed to be free. Children should not be prostituted. It's not far from believing that children owe affection for gifts to believing that they should go to bed with someone for an ice cream cone or for a drink in a bar or to get and keep love and attention.

Some people say the child consented, but children cannot give consent. They must depend upon and trust adults for protection and guidance. If an adult makes a suggestion or a demand, why would a child question its appropriateness? Children are used to obeying their elders. Consent and responsibility can only come from understanding the consequences and having the power to refuse.


**Naomi Seiko Yamasaka:** I was born in Osaka, Japan, and lived in a Catholic orphanage until I was two and a half when I was adopted by an American couple. Now 37 and a lesbian, I've lived in several states in the U.S. I sculpt, dance and travel. Presently I work in the social services.

The incident I have described happened after my adopted mother died and I was put into a children's home. I also am a survivor of eight years of child molest by my adopted father. The reason I chose a milder incident than what my father did was to show that molest is not sex.

# Gang-Rape in D.C. Jail

On the afternoon of August 21, 1973, i was called into the Captain's Office of the ancient (100-year-old) District of Columbia Jail in eastern Washington. I was awaiting trial, being held on $10 bail, on a charge of trespass for participating in a pray-in on the White House lawn in connection with the bombing of Cambodia. (i was eventually acquitted by jury.) I had refused to post bail in protest against racial and class discrimination in the bail system. I had been in the D.C. Jail for a week, in a very quiet section reserved for old men and the few whites (like G. Gordon Liddy) in the jail. During this time staff had urged me a couple of times to post bail and leave. They didn't want a young newspaper reporter (for that was my occupation) in the jail at a time when riots were a weekly occurrence (two happened in other sections while i was in the quiet area). Anyway, the Captain, Clinton Cobb, called me in and told me i was threatened with sexual assault in the area where i was. I told him this was not apparent to me. He urged me to leave or go into solitary confinement for my own protection. I refused. Then he said "I'm going to transfer you for your protection to Cell Block Two." I didn't know at that time that C.B.2 was one of the two roughest cellblocks in the whole jail. Lt. Sutphin was present at this discussion.

Captain Cobb's subsequent "cover-your-ass" memo of the 24th (reprinted in G. Gordon Liddy's book *Will*) asserted that an Officer E. Todd on the 22nd (the day after i had been transferred) reported that due to "an unusual amount of inmate traffic around" my cell, he "suspected, although he could not substantiate the fact" that if i "remained in the Unit, [i] would be attacked by numerous inmates." This is, even if truly reported in Cobb's memo, hardly sufficient to place me in C.B.2 with its known dangers. It's a cover-up for a set-up.

I was taken into C.B.2, five long tiers of cages facing a wall with windows and blaring TV and radio sets mounted on it. The ground floor was used for feeding and had tables for chess, etc. At first i was locked into a cell on the second tier, which was the second furthest cell from the guard post. The guards didn't routinely enter the cellblock for fear of being assaulted themselves, as they admitted to reporters afterward. At first i thought i was in solitary, since other prisoners were out walking the catwalks around the tiers. Some of them stopped to talk to me. One was a 19-year-old black named "Baseball" who asked a lot of questions, where i was from, why i was in there, etc. I told him about the White House pray-in and my pacifist convictions.

At suppertime I was let out to eat, and Baseball approached me again, offering to give me some LSD. I declined. I milled around for a bit on the ground floor trying to take in the place. Everyone around me was black, some 200 in the cellblock. There was one other white boy in C.B.2, but i never got to talk to him.

After chow time came what is called "indoor recreation period" when guys can go down to the ground floor, from 7 til 11. I was standing on the ground floor around 7:30 p.m. when one tall dude came up to me and started asking me if it were true that i was a Quaker pacifist, said he had heard about the pray-in at the White House. I talked freely with him, having no fear. He then said, "There be some dudes wanna talk wit' you" back in one of the cells, would i go with him. I was eager to explain Quaker principles and naive and innocent, so i followed him off the open area onto the first tier (which was at ground floor level) and into the last cell (furthest away from the guards). Cops could see along the walkway but not into the cells, which were at right angles to them.

There were several guys already in the cell, and several more followed me in. One of them was Baseball. I said "What do you want to talk about?" Ignoring the question, one of the big guys said "Take your pants off!" "Like hell!" said i, and looked around, but the cell door was blocked.

"Are you gonna cooperate or do we gotta get rough?"

"I may not be able to stop you, but i sure as hell ain't gonna help you!" Now i was trembling. Then they grabbed me. They picked me up and rammed my head against the metal railing of the top bunk several times, then set me down on the toilet bowl in the far corner of the little cell. I was dazed, the place was spinning.

When my vision cleared, i saw Baseball standing in front of me with a hard dick jutting out towards me like a battleship's gun.

"If you bite anybody, or if you say one word about this to the

Man," he threatened, "you'll be dead, and there ain't no place in this motherfuckin' jail we can't get to you, so you better do what you're told." Right next to and behind him were about five other guys. Then he thrust his dick against my lips. Dick smell assaulted my nostrils, and a feeling of revulsion ran down my spine. I was trembling noticeably. But i refused to open my mouth. I wasn't going to help in any way; passive resistance seemed to be the path to take in face of such odds.

Then Baseball punched me in the head. Through the pain i realized that this would continue until they got what they wanted, and i could suffer permanent injury without them thinking twice about it. So mentally i surrendered.

He pressed his dick against my lips again and made a fist; i slowly and reluctantly opened my mouth and he shoved his dick into it. How can i describe how it felt? Humiliation, anger, helplessness, amazement, strangeness, weirdness, this-isn't-really-happening-to-me, the overwhelming presence of Power, racial guilt, etc. all ran through my mind very quickly.

He pressed in til i started gagging, which was pretty quickly. I heaved out my guts into the toilet bowl, then he came back and started fucking my mouth again, holding my head in a viselike grip from which there was no escaping. When he shot off, i was amazed. He kept my head down into his crotch after he came until i swallowed his cum, then he let me up. The crotch smell was very strong, with my nose pressed up against his pubic hair. I looked up and he was smiling in triumph.

I was scared to death but hopeful that it would all be over in a few minutes and that they wouldn't hurt me any more since they were getting what they wanted. I also hoped it would just be Baseball, but as soon as he stepped away, another guy took his place, unzipped and brought out another dark peter which he forced between my lips. In this way five guys fucked me in the mouth, one after another. They came off pretty quickly for the most part.

I was then lifted off the toilet bowl and told to take my pants off, for the second time. Again, i refused, but i was helpless; they just pulled them off me, picked me up and placed me belly-down on the bottom bunk. A guy climbed on top of me and tried to get his dick in me, but it wouldn't go, so he called out to get some "grease" and a minute later stuck his finger in me with some lubricant on it. I was being held down all this time with a pillow over my head. Then the guy tried again and finally managed to get the head of his dick into my asshole, then pushed real hard. "Got me a real sweet cherry!" he said. It hurt enormously and i cried out involuntarily, then somebody stuffed a towel in my mouth. The guy fucked me hard and muttered to himself. My arms were pinned along my sides and he was squeezing me very tight. Then he got up and another guy got on me and fucked me, but he was slower and took his time about it. The other guys got restless at this. It didn't hurt as bad as the first guy.

When he got off, the guy whose cell i was in asked Baseball to move the show somewhere else. They checked to see if anyone was watching from the guard post and then dragged me to the next cell over.

Until about 10 p.m. i kept getting fucked in the mouth and ass and dragged from one cell to another down the first tier after about every five guys. Baseball and a friend of his were collecting cigarettes—two packs for a crack at me.

One guy had an enormous dick, it must have been at least five inches in diameter. I told him, when he stepped up to me, "You'll kill me with that!" He argued with me, and i pleaded and begged him not to try it. I couldn't believe anyone had a dick that big. Finally, he sighed and turned and walked out. I don't know if he got his cigarettes back.

My fear became pure panic, as there was no end in sight. My ass and my jaw were in tremendous pain, and my head still ached from the beating it had taken.

A lot of guys had me get down on my knees while they fucked my mouth. I wouldn't do anything voluntarily, so they all had to hold my head and force it up and down on their dicks. I must have swallowed a quart of cum. The rest had me sit on the toilet bowl when they took my mouth. Most of them got head since whenever somebody wanted my ass i begged them to take my head instead (it didn't hurt as much) and most of them obliged.

Some of the guys were very rough and were obviously taking out their anger and frustration on me. One of them told me "Your ass belongs to the black man and don't you forget it!" Others would whisper stuff in my ear and call me by female names and kiss the back of my neck or lick my earlobe while they were fucking my ass. Some of them stayed on top of me a while after they came. That didn't hurt, so i welcomed it as a change from the constant thrusting. It gave me a chance to contemplate the situation i was in and the feeling of having that powerful body covering me up from head to toe, with his male organ stuck deep up my ass. I wondered if this was how women felt when i fucked them. I felt totally helpless, overpowered. I no longer had any responsibility for what happened to my body. Often i abandoned my body mentally and withdrew into my head. Sometimes i tried to imagine how it felt to the other guy to be fucking me and wondered why he would do that. Sometimes i thought they would kill me after they were finished with me.

I came to identify the hard cock that was so irresistibly, relentlessly and repeatedly invading my body with the personification of Power. It was like a wrathful god of ancient days, demanding obedience and exacting punishment for the least resistance, awesome and uncannily incomprehensible in its power, and i was the human sacrifice. I went into altered states of consciousness spontaneously. Sometimes i felt like a slave, sometimes felt like i was paying for all the sins of the white race against the blacks, the sacrificial lamb. Sometimes i paid attention to the technical details of what got a guy off the fastest, what tongue movement did the trick, how the cut and uncut dicks reacted differently. Sometimes i was most aware of the visual aspect, the huge organs pointed straight at my face, looking up to see the towering glistening bodies (it was hot and most were shirtless) like skyscrapers over me. Sometimes it was the smell of dick and crotch that occupied my attention, sometimes the feeling of the hard abdominal muscles of the guys pressing against my nose and forehead, sometimes the different tastes of dick and semen.

Sometimes i just wondered, why me? Why did so many guys want me? What was it about me that made their dicks hard and made them want to take me? I knew i was boyish and good-looking, but now i seemed to have become a magnet for every dick in the neighborhood.

Around 10 p.m. i was taken to the big shower room, which also could not be seen by the guards outside the block. Here, amidst the swirling steam, they made me get down on all fours and fucked me in the mouth and ass at the same time. I was in agonizing pain, every thrust was an ordeal. I prayed endlessly for it to end, but it seemed like i was condemned to an eternity of painful dicks. I could

63

hear the guys laughing and joking about me.

When there was a break—about 45 guys had fucked me by now—Baseball walked over and pointed his dick at me, but it was soft; i couldn't figure out what he wanted. Then i was startled to see a stream of piss coming out of his dick at me, and feeling it run all over my body, very warm. He played his dick like a hose all over my back and ass. It was a real strange feeling. I couldn't be any more humiliated than i already was; my mental processes were long since stripped down to the basic level, so mostly i just felt the warm water running down my side and legs.

There were about 15 dudes in the shower room at this time, and they were all watching. When Baseball finished, two more stepped up and started pissing on me. Almost immediately still another came around and stood in front of me. He pulled on my hair to raise my head, and ordered me to open my mouth. For a couple of minutes we were frozen like that, me staring at his soft dick pointing at me and him looking down at me. Then he started pissing right into my mouth. "Drink my piss, white boy!" he said with a fierce low voice. It was all i could do to get it down. "I got a new job for you, punk," he said, "you're gonna be the piss-bowl for every nigger that feels like savin' hisself a few steps."

It dawned on me that this was at least not painful—nobody was fucking me anymore, and the piss didn't hurt. So i relaxed and actually welcomed the relief from the pain that was driving me crazy. I thought it was their way of showing who was the boss, and marking off their property. When he was finished, others took his place. I couldn't keep swallowing piss cause my belly was soon full up, and i just let it run out of my mouth. Others pissed on my body. When i realized nobody was fucking my ass, i collapsed on the tile floor. Baseball told me to roll over, and kicked me til i did, then they pissed on my belly and dick and face and into my mouth. It was weird looking up and seeing these towering black figures and the steam swirling around them and all these dicks pointing at me and the piss streaming out of them onto me. For a while i just closed my eyes, but Baseball made me keep them open when he noticed it. At least they didn't piss in my eyes.

When everybody was finished, they turned the water on me and washed me off, gave me my pants to put back on, and led me to a cell—not my own, but they had arranged a switch so that i was put in a two-man cell with another guy. After the count (they made me pull a blanket over my face so the cop couldn't see i was white) the guy on the top bunk came down and crawled on top of me. I pleaded with him not to fuck me, telling him how painful it was. He said he'd be real quick, cause he didn't want to hurt me, but he was still determined to fuck me so he did. He did come off very soon, and then lay on top of me for a long, long time, it must have been at least an hour. He had his arms around me and licked my ears and tried to calm me down. I was crying uncontrollably and continued for a long time; until then i had been too terrorized to weep. He said he knew it was rough, but that was just how the new kids were welcomed to the block on the first day and it would be different after that. To that slender reed of hope i clung.

When i totally surrendered my body to these rapists, i discovered that in the midst of all that pain and terror, it was in some very undescribable way totally relaxing. I had abandoned myself to my fate, had ceased to struggle.

Sometimes i had no sense at all that what was happening was sexual; there was just the awesome reality and power of this hard warm object in my mouth or ass. i stopped thinking of it as a dick or what it was doing as fucking; it was just there and never-ending, the dominant feature of my universe.

The next morning i returned to my own cell and stayed there except for outdoor yard and a visit and chow. Baseball insisted i eat at his table but didn't talk to me and let nobody else talk to me. One guy stopped me on my way back to my cell and asked if i'd let him fuck me, but he didn't want to rape me. I told him "I ain't about to volunteer" and he turned away, disappointed, but telling me to let him know if i changed my mind.

When the "indoor recreation period" began that evening, the 22nd, i stayed in my cell and tried to write a letter. This was interrupted when Baseball and his buddies arrived and invaded my cell. He pushed me down onto my knees and grabbed my hair and pulled my head into his crotch and made me suck his dick. I was in no condition to resist. Then his partner got his dick sucked, and several more guys, and some fucked me. Baseball and his partner came back again and again, telling the other dudes to watch them as they fucked my face. After coming off about four times or so, they couldn't get it hard again but still wanted me to suck them in front of their friends. That didn't arouse much interest from the audience, so they then tried pissing into my mouth. They said, "The brothers can make this punk drink your piss anytime you want, but don't skeet [shoot off] til you see me first."

I was in even more of a panic this second night because my hopes had been dashed that there would be an end to it. I could only see endless pain for hours every day. My mind descended to the animal level of pure instinct and survival.

When some of the dudes kept fucking me in the mouth, i gagged and threw up. Then they let me sit on the bottom bunk for a while, with my pants off. This was about 10 p.m., and i'd had about 15 guys rape me that evening, most several times. The guys had gotten careless and the door to the cell was not blocked, so when i heard a lookout on the catwalk say "Hey, the Man's watching," i reacted without thinking and dove headfirst out the door on to the catwalk, picked myself up and ran like hell down the catwalk to the end, where a guard opened the gate and let me out. Then i collapsed, sobbing, on the floor, naked.

One of the guards there told me "You were set up" (by Captain Cobb). They sent me to the jail infirmary where i spent an awful night, without so much as aspirin, interrupted by a handcuffed visit to D.C. General Hospital for cursory examination, during which I was treated as a contemptible criminal. (Injury to my ass later necessitated surgery and hospitalization.)

The next day i was bailed out after calling a Quaker friend. There was a press conference at Quaker House—being a journalist, this seemed natural to me—and that's how the story got out. I was the first victim of jail rape to speak out about it in public. It was all over the newspapers (*The Washington Star-News* called editorially for the resignation of the head of the jail) and on all the TV stations and has been described in Susan Brownmiller's *Against Our Will*, Anthony Scacco's *Male Rape* and Liddy's *Will*, though not in such detail as here.

There were City Council hearings and a grand jury investigation, but nothing actually changed. Cobb was transferred and promoted; Baseball was killed in prison in 1977. (Karma!)

This experience turned my life upside down. Fourteen years later, it still haunts me, and i'm still trying to fathom its meaning, spiritually and otherwise, for i've never "gotten over it," and probably never will. But i did survive and gained a new mission in life as a result.

\* \* \* \*

The person who answered the D.C. Rape Hotline when i called was not interested in male victims, a response which has proved all too common in my subsequent years of activism on the issue of rape of males, my own major area of social concern. It took 3 years for me to get even low-level counseling. My rage erupted non-sexually in a hospital emergency room in 1980. Although no one was injured, this led to my spending 4 years in federal prison, where rape was routine, institutionalized and adapted to.

After my release, i received formal training as a peer counselor for rape survivors at St. Vincent's Hospital in New York City, becoming co-coordinator of the men's counselor group of the Rape Crisis Program there. Then St. Vincent's decided to abandon the male part of the program on the grounds that it was diverting staff time and energy away from their priority: women. I went on to organize and chair a Committee on Male Survivors of Rape under the New York City Task Force Against Sexual Assault and also ran into resistance from many women over including males among the concerns of the anti-rape movement.

Recent research has shown that boys and girls are at equal risk of sexual assault and that most adult male rapists are themselves untreated survivors of sexual assault.[1] This is a vicious cycle, indeed, and it is fed by the lack of counseling for male victims and by the idea that rape is solely a problem for females or is a "woman's issue" only, an idea still being propagated by much, if not most, of the anti-rape movement. The women in the anti-rape movement are still demonstrating marked reluctance in deed and often in word to come to terms with the many issues posed by the victimization of males and its consequences, issues largely evaded and avoided. As long as this continues, the vicious cycle will also continue to claim ever more victims among females and males. I can only hope that this piece helps break the ice.

**Robert A. Martin:** I am currently president of People Organized to Stop the Rape of Incarcerated Persons (POSRIP) and am known by my pen name Stephen Donaldson. The U.S. Parole Commission has prohibited me from discussing jail and prisons on radio and television; they are afraid of the truth, and do not want it discussed. And you, dear reader?

[1] Eugene Porter, *Treating the Young Male Victim of Sexual Assault* (Syracuse, N.Y.: Safer Society Press, 1986).

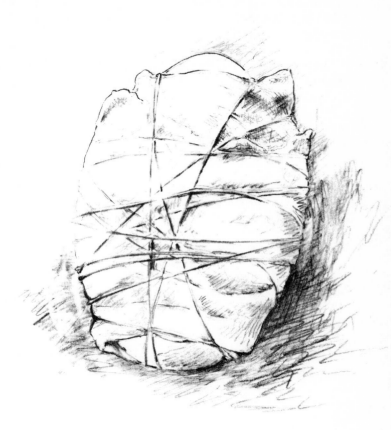

# Consequences

# Silent Panic

The threads
That are holding me
Together
Are stretched so taut
That
Pieces of them
Are already
Frayed and
Broken,
And I am
Afraid
That when the last
String
Breaks,
All that's left of me
Will come apart
And go careening off
Into the universe
And be
Lost
Forever.

**Sally Kay Emerich:** One night in June of 1983, after 23 years of silence, my parents and I finally talked about my molest. (The perpetrator was our gardener.) This poem, written last year, expresses my response to emotional pain and separation, the universal legacy of permanent scars left on the hearts of sexually molested children.

I have learned in the past four years that we must accept and work through the anger and the pain; we cannot obliterate it. For me, writing poetry has been a part of that grieving process; and grieve we must, in order to go on. And we do go on.

Our success lies in realizing our power to direct our futures. At 39, I am finding my personal power through writing, educating and developing healthy relationships with people, focusing always on honesty, integrity, personal responsibility and love, with acceptance and forgiveness for myself and all of humanity.

# Journal Excerpts

I always have a sense of loss, of grieving. I feel that I am a case history somewhat separate from myself. I put too much emphasis on it, I should be able to let it go and at the same time I don't want to let it go. It is my identity and if I let it go, I will disappear. I'm afraid I will bore or annoy the psychiatrist by going on and on about it. What makes me go on about it is that I really want to scream, WILL SOMEONE PLEASE HELP THAT LITTLE GIRL, yet I have a hard time feeling that that little girl is me. I feel her pain constantly, yet I am separate from her. I see her, I don't see me. Maybe I don't exist. I am so afraid of feeling sorry for myself. Recently I have come to feel pity for that child, not for me.

I can't shake the feeling that I am damaged. I have somehow managed to lead a normal life but it was something that happened to me, not something that I had control over. I feel that because I have led an outwardly normal life, I am not entitled to be in such pain. I try constantly to hide the pain, the depression, finding other reasons for being unhappy. I hide beneath a veneer of strength, efficiency, humor ("mirth is the mail of anguish"—Emily Dickinson). When I read other case histories, I find comfort. Someone else feels as I do, feels the scream inside. But so many others had a much harder time, violence, so therefore I do not feel entitled to my pain. When I am happy, it doesn't feel comfortable, I know it's only temporary, not really me, a costume I put on to please others. If I lived alone and didn't have to worry about others, I would be free to feel bad all the time. I am trapped inside myself.

There is always the need to be careful, not reveal myself. On guard constantly. If you have to keep one secret, you have to keep everything secret. Even from yourself—no wonder I do not know myself. Hide, hide, hide. High necks, long sleeves, avoid community dressing rooms, take quick showers, never baths. Never expose yourself, your body might reveal your secret.

73

I am a transient in life—never fitting in, belonging nowhere. Soiled, tainted, unsavory. Does it show? Do I look like a victim? Is there a mark on me, a sign? Victim for Rent. Rent-A-Victim. By the hour, by the day, by the lifetime.

I am so ashamed of everything I do, everything I say, everything I want. Everything I do is all wrong. I know it's sick, no one can be as bad as I feel I am. Sometimes it is such an effort to live. Is it worth it? Why does everyone think life is so precious? I wouldn't mind dying. At times only responsibility keeps me from suicide. My body hurts all the time, a container for pain, a grey blob of impacted pain. Maybe that's why I eat so much—trying to dislodge the blob.

Terrible session today. Remembered what it felt like. That incredibly smooth thing working itself between my legs. I suspend myself, terrified, waiting to see what is going to happen. Want to scream and cry but good little girls don't cry. Where is my mother?

Did my mother know? And knowing, condone? Was she punishing me? For being a girl, for being prettier than her, for being born, for not eating my spinach? So confused. Is this another rule I don't understand but must obey, like going to bed even though the sun is still shining! What happens now?

I am so frightened. I build a playpen of safety using "shoulds" and "mustn'ts" as barriers to life. An emotional girdle holds me in check. I fear the release, the expansion. Wanton feelings float to the surface. I am so tired, all I want to do is sleep. Lethargy is comforting, deathlike.

I yearn to dance, but dancing is sensual, provocative, to be avoided. If I shake my ass, someone might climb up on it. The need to move to the music is unbearable. How can I, encased in a head to toe girdle?

Was I better off before I remembered? Remembered today how he came up behind me when I was sixteen, his pajamas gaping, flaccid, sick grin on his face. Violent feelings in stomach. Push down. Can't. I HATE YOU, YOU FUCKING SON OF A BITCH. I

74

NEEDED YOU. I LOVED YOU. I TRUSTED YOU.

There are still blank spots. I remember four years old, I remember six years old, nine years old, and I remember finally pushing him away at sixteen. I guess it's not important to remember it all. I am getting better, the blob is beginning to shift. I don't feel so futile. I don't actually see the light at the end of the tunnel but I know that it is there.

I know now that it wasn't my fault. The shame is theirs, not mine. They did it to me. Why do I say "they" not "he"? Because incest involves more than the two participants. A conspiracy exists that allows it to occur. Adults are powerful, all seeing. (Didn't my mother always see my fibs written on my forehead?) Therefore, the child believes they are aware of what is happening to her, what she is doing and interprets their silence as approval. That is her reality. But since she knows intuitively incest is wrong and adults know right from wrong, their assent endangers her reality.

**Norma Rothstein:** I was thirty-two years old when memories of what my "loving" grandfather had done to me began surfacing. During the healing process, journal keeping gave me a place to scream in private, but as I recorded my progress from victim to survivor, writing itself become very important to me and evolved from a therapeutic to a creative process. I now write full time, take myself seriously as a writer and hope one day to see my work published. I am determined to give this survivor's story a happy ending. I know I won't stop trying.

# Inhale

BREATHE . . .

gulps of air
there a deep breath
filling my lungs—
but pain spills out
blocking, blocking.
Anger as I hold her near,
almost curled fists
tightening, tightening.

BREATHE . . .

let the air in,
let the warmth in,
feel the pain.
The knot stuck there,
tight threads, choking,
stuck in my throat
surrounding my heart.

BREATHE . . .

she tells me and I do,
claiming space
easing the threads.
We tug at them slowly,
they start to unravel.
Letting go of my uncle's
presence in my life.
Exhaling all the rage
of my father when he found out.

Inhaling.

**Thelma Stoudt:** I was seven when I was abused. At 32 I am amazed at the process required for me to acknowledge the abuse's effects on my life. With the help of friends, other survivors' writings, drop-in groups, therapy and my lover, I have learned to appreciate my strength as a survivor. Currently, I am back in college, am working at a collective mailing firm and recently was trained as a literacy tutor. I am interested in feminism and nonviolence, herbs, eco-feminism and education that empowers. I am working class. This poem was written for my lover, Judy.

# A Habit of Wounding

Diving into my own body
the scent of silver blue
on my skin
a field of poppies
like those Gwennie brought me
drooping stems
a womb on each
lime green stalk
a burst of blood
or miniature hearts.

The smothering
of all that was
too sweet to hold
the way spring ached
so peculiar to Scotland
the bitter black soil
sweetened by
bleeding delicate green wounds
in the brown rug of brush.

Oh, it's like
the blood of virgins
only I did not bleed
the first time
it was years later
as pain became habitual.

**Lucie Work:** The power that men have over women, and my belief that this was inevitable, led me into several violent relationships in which I felt powerless to change. As a writer, pain and wounding became almost comfortable subjects. As women, we are not encouraged to express ourselves openly or honestly. After a "good" education, I was still unable to articulate what I *knew* into what I *felt* and did. Being in violent situations allowed others to act out my violence and anger for me, while I remained "a good girl." Now, several years and a wonderful marriage later, the love and trust my friends have shown me have allowed me to feel safe in expressing myself fully as a woman and as a writer.

# Rabbit Slaughter

Unlucky hind feet
he uses to hold
you upside
down,

then with one board blow
to neck—you stiffen,
not crying
out.

Only one single
THUD, swallowed by dull
November
trees.

I flinch, thinking of
how I have likewise
been struck by
him.

As your black-red blood
spills, I count all the
times mine has
flowed.

With his steady strong
hands he slits down your
belly just
once,

slips pelt off easy,
undressing you, now
leaving you
naked.

Like his, your light smooth
skin on the leaved floor,
so reminds
me.

His knife cuts your chest.
I watch, pretending
instead it's
his.


**Teresa Imfeld:** I grew up in southwestern Ohio but have also lived in Washington State and Missouri. I now make my home in San Francisco, California. In addition to printed pieces (poems, stories, etc.), I am fascinated with performance. My present goal is to incorporate music and movement into my work.

When I wrote the final draft of "Rabbit Slaughter," I was frightened by the violence in it. I had kept my feelings in check for so long that when I finally unleashed them, I could not believe how powerful they were, nor how strongly I had denied them.

# You Have Been Dying for Me

I saw you murdered this morning
after you left to camp in Reddington Pass.
For an hour I handled the senseless killing
with fiendish grief, sobbed relentlessly
in someone's arms, allowing myself to be
comforted and thoroughly weak.
When finally I could stop the cremation,
the memorial service, my life sprouting wildly
without you, my guilt grew as detailed
as my fantasies of these rugs
on different floors, the same dirty dishes in the sink.

This isn't the first time you've died in my fantasies.
Only your death, my husband, could justify
the magnitude of the grief I cannot release.
I have to imagine you dead to mourn for me.

Why is grief appropriate for husbands
but not for lost selves?
What of the child running home at dusk,
being tickled by her brother in the one-bulb-bright
living room, crying as at an omen?
Did something forgotten happen nights in that house
where a hurricane fence in the backyard sealed off
the sharp brush roamed by packs
of domesticated dogs gone wild?

Still lacking the words to say
how a familiar doorjamb changes
when the door opens at night,
I learned what rape meant at eight.
Explaining to a friend in the fifth grade
that babies do not come from under cabbage leaves,
I had lived with the fear of pregnancy

82

since nine when I began bleeding and thought
my insides where falling out.

To cry for the child my brother ruptured
inside me is hard,
after living a lifetime without her.
A smart child, she knew many things:
that insomnia was vigilance;
that fear was a red flag, disguised
as a dark sound to snap her awake;
that being numb as the floor
meant not strangling on nightmares in the daytime;
that living inside herself inside the room
no longer hers after dark was safer
than trusting anyone;
that silence was life then.
In learning these she lost other things,
like the fascinating taste of pennies in the mouth,
things no one ever looked for or missed.
I must admire, not only the A's she made at school,
repeatedly, to prove her worth to me,
but her capacity for survival,
swallowing terror like a lump in the throat,
quietly, with no glass of water beside the bed.

In a dream last night a twelve-year-old girl told me:
*Women want to be accepted for themselves.*
I wake with a tightening pain in my colon,
the spot pierced if we make love carelessly.
I hear a sound in the kitchen and wake you.
Naked, you walk uncomplaining through the house,
checking in the closets, beneath the desk,
behind the shower curtain, appeasing my fear
of disaster that comes from within.
I tell you my dream and you say:
*Perhaps she is you as a child speaking,*
*at twelve, as the adult you had to be.*
Grief fills me like the cracks in an old tongue-and-groove floor,
imperfectly, in the no-longer-impervious wood, that is me,
in your arms, on your chest, as six tears roll down my cheeks.

In the morning I will begin dreaming you dead,

and I will hate my brother for this,
when I remember how anger feels.


**Pamela Portwood**: In 1983, I first understood the relationship of incest and rape to my many recurrent problems after reading "Untitled Incest Piece," a personal essay by Anne Lee published in *Voices in the Night: Women Speaking About Incest*.[1] After two years of attending support groups, of going through therapy, of reading, writing and editing poetry and prose on sexual violence, I confronted my brother and parents with the incest. Despite my brother's denials, my parents courageously believed me.

Now, four years after the first time I saw the word "incest" in print as something other than an anthropological, literary or historical rarity, the taboo and the rapists have lost their power over me. Finally, I feel a whole and complete human being rather than a flawed, perverse and powerless child. Yet I could never thank Anne Lee for providing the catalyst that changed my life because she died of cancer in 1981. Instead, I hope to return to others through *Rebirth of Power* her gift of words and insight to me.


[1]Anne Lee, "Untitled Incest Piece" in Toni A. H. McNaron and Yarrow Morgan, ed., *Voices in the Night: Women Speaking About Incest* (Minneapolis: Cleis Press, 1982), pp. 165-171.

# The Swimmer

## I

They sent her to stay with her aunt and uncle, north of San Francisco, and for a month her mother neither wrote nor called: she could not bring herself to make a contact, even to tell a lie that might begin the healing.

The late winter and early spring mornings smoked with fog, and Maureen felt as if it had flowed into her head and stayed there. She went to school half-asleep and ate, half-asleep, then went to her room and listened to Josh White on the phonograph. Mrs. Ord, her aunt, tried to get her to eat more and turn off the phonograph and the light earlier, because she thought she needed sleep. She scolded her mildly about her room being a mess, and begged her not to start smoking, because it was a habit she would never afterward be able to break. Maureen responded to it all like a sleepwalker, so that Mrs. Ord finally took her to the doctor. He recommended more sleep and bigger meals, and told her smoking would stunt her growth. Maureen replied that she had never wanted to be very big, anyway, and the doctor had stiffened.

The Ords knew something had happened in Michigan. Maureen's mother had not talked to her sister either, but Mrs. Ord knew. There was bound to be something strange about an inventor; and then if you married one, what did you expect? Of course, Mrs. Ord's sister Stella was a strange one herself: she had gone through men—and strange men at that—like a movie queen. So something had happened, and somehow it had fallen upon the child. And of course the Ords did not want to know the details—what good would that have done?

The Lord had willed that they should have no children of their own, and they had resigned themselves to the fact. But it was their Christian duty to help the needy in any way they could, and when it was your own sister's only child, all the more. Only they wished she weren't quite so strange, and did not keep her room in such unspeakable chaos. Maybe all teenage girls were strange and messy; they believed this and tried to be patient and understanding, but Maureen was enough to try the forbearance of a saint: she was so—remote, somehow.

Maureen's mother wrote, finally. She and Eliot had separated, and she did not think she would ever marry again. She had discovered a wonderful religion based on a belief in reincarnation which would require a lifetime of study and meditation. All she wanted to do now was to live alone in the mountains somewhere, and find herself. She didn't know if Maureen could ever forgive her, but she was certain she could never forgive herself.

Summer came, and there was a pool, and mostly the afternoons were hot, and that made up for almost everything. The pool was always crowded, filled with yelling, splashing kids, the chlorine burned her eyes, the pool manager and the ticket taker ordered everybody around and snarled at anyone who broke a rule like showering before swimming or wearing a bathing cap. (Maureen had had her hair cut very short that spring, like a boy's, and so didn't really need a cap: but they yelled at her anyway, because every girl had to wear one.) If the lifeguard was a boy, he whistled at her and made eyes every chance he got; if it was a girl, she either pretended Maureen didn't exist or gave her dirty looks, as though Maureen had done her an injury.

Still the pool was almost paradise. Maureen could shut out the voices and the prying eyes and swim and swim, lap after lap, smoothly, rhythmically—perfectly, it seemed to her. She lost herself in pure motion and the flow of the warm water along her sides. She became aware of others only when someone blundered into her and broke the rhythm.

She went home in the afternoon red-eyed and slack-limbed and happy.

But her aunt and uncle worried about the swimming, too, because it seemed an obsession. There were plenty of girls her age who had jobs waitressing in drive-ins or clerking in department stores, to earn a little pin money. It wasn't that she needed the money, of course, but it was a way of training herself to manage, later in life.

So Maureen put on her plainest brown blouse and skirt, and landed a cashier's job in a drugstore. At first she made mistakes because she was absent-minded. She got over that, though the druggist watched her constantly, as if she were a thief, and so made her nervous. But then it turned out she frowned too much, and made the customers uncomfortable, so she was ordered to smile as she made change.  Then Maureen concentrated on the smiling, and somehow caught her hand in the automatically-locking drawer of the cash register, so that the druggist had to send for a repairman to dismantle the machine in order to free her.  And though Maureen tried to smile the whole time, this was too much for the druggist, who gave her a check and sent her home.

She went to the pool again, but it wasn't the same.  The screaming kids, the gawking lifeguards, the chlorine—everything broke in on her.  Because they wanted her to *do* something—her aunt and uncle did.  They worked every day, Mr. Ord as a book-keeper in a fish-processing plant and Mrs. Ord as a florist's assis-tant, and they hated it when Maureen slept until eleven o'clock and then went to the pool until five and came home red-eyed.  Even though she tried to be agreeable and cooperative always, she offended them, deep down.  She could see their eyes narrow and their mouths set.  And she heard them, too, through the thin walls, when they thought she was asleep.

"Well, she's had all spring, Harriet.  Maybe she just isn't any good.  There're kids like that, now you know there are.  Just no good."

"Oh, Bill, she's just a child, and all alone—"

"She's big enough to have every male on the street ogling her—don't tell me.  I *see* it."

"But she can't help that—"

"No?  Well it takes two to tango, Harriet, I always say."

"Besides, something happened to her, back there in Michigan.  She got hurt somehow, and it's made her, I don't know—strange—not normal."

"And you think she didn't invite it?  Well, you won't convince me.  She may be our niece, but there's something spoiled about that girl, deep inside.  And everybody knows it—everybody."

"Well, maybe you're right.  You're awfully good at figuring people out.  But I can't help wondering—the poor little thing."

For weeks now Maureen had shut out every thought about what had happened in Michigan.  She had stayed numb, like a sleepwalker.  Only sometimes, just as she shut off the light and lay back to go to sleep truly, it would come at her, like a terror whose source she could no longer name, and she would break out into a sweat.  Then for the next few nights she would postpone putting out the light as long as she could, dreading the first moment of darkness, because the terror lived in it.

Now she thought about being spoiled inside. Maybe her uncle was right. He was much older than she was, and had known a lot of people, so maybe he knew. The way her stepfather had looked at her, and the lifeguards, and even men on the street she didn't know—maybe it wasn't in them, but in her. Maybe they couldn't help themselves, maybe they were like dogs drawn irresistibly to garbage. Her aunt and uncle wanted to help her—they had told her so repeatedly—so maybe they hadn't told her about herself because they didn't want to hurt her.

Then Maureen began remembering images, at any odd hour of the day: a moustache, a figured carpet, a square-cut whiskey bottle, the fat warm radio. And sometimes they would be mixed: there would be the radio, glowing, but bristling as if it were covered all over with hair. She did not think about her mother at all.

She determined to be good: she would please her aunt and uncle and make the images go away. She would be perfect, and not spend all her time in the pool anymore, and everybody would love her.

When she went to look for jobs in the other stores in town, though, it seemed there weren't any. Even where there was a help-wanted sign in the window they told her they already had someone, and had meant to take the sign down. She noticed they didn't take the signs down, though: it was a very small town and the druggist had talked to everyone.

Finally she got a job at the Gold Coast Drive-in, serving hamburgers and fries and milk shakes, mostly to kids around her own age, from four o'clock until midnight. But the boys all hounded her, and then made fun of her when she wouldn't respond. She seemed to take their propositions in stride and ignore them, and that drove them wild. Some of the older ones would roar away in their hot rods and then come back, smelling of beer. They would grip her wrist at the car window, to make her stand there, while they told her all the things they were going to do to her when she tried to go home. And in fact, one night a carload of them did follow her, all eight blocks to her uncle's house, calling to her and finally calling her names, when she wouldn't respond.

Then when she went into her bedroom she was afraid to turn off the light, because she knew the images would come; and the next day she quit her job at the drive-in, and the manager was very angry.

She tried a couple of other jobs after that—ushering in the local theater, packing tomatoes—but something went wrong each time. She made mistakes, because she couldn't concentrate. She kept seeing the images—mustache, rug, empty swimming pool with leaves swirled in it, the bristling radio. She wanted to talk to her aunt and uncle, to ask them what was wrong with her, inside, because she wanted to be good, she really did, and she couldn't. But more and more they acted as if she didn't exist, or as if they wished she would disappear. Her uncle scarcely looked up from his paper when she came in, and if she went to her aunt in the kitchen, she told Maureen that she was busy and that Maureen had better go to her room. It was as though they hated her, just when she was trying hardest to be good.

For some time Maureen had known a part-Mexican girl named Rosie who lived on the bad side of town and went out with older men and knew how to make them give her wine. Rosie was always asking her if she wanted to walk out under the railroad bridge, and drink wine. But Maureen knew Rosie wasn't a nice girl, in spite of her warm brown skin and black eyes, and that her aunt and uncle would be very angry with her if they knew she had gone with Rosie, so she had always refused.

But the day Maureen lost her job at the tomato-packing plant she was sitting on the curb, her blouse and jeans spattered with tomato juice, the woman foreman's words still ringing in her ears, when Rosie happened along—Rosie who had not even tried to work all summer, who said that that was what men were for—and offered her a cigarette. Maureen took it, and they sat on the curb, smoking.

"I've got something wrong with me, inside," Maureen said.

"You mean like cancer?"

"No."

Rosie looked her up and down. "Well you sure look O.K. to *me*. If I had your looks, I'd be rich, you bet."

They lapsed into silence, smoking.

"These are a good brand," Rosie said, holding up the cigarette. "My boyfriend Alex, that works in the Standard station, he buys 'em for me."

"What are they?" Maureen said, without looking.

"Luckies."

"It's a nice name. I thought that the first time I smoked one."

"We could drink some wine with them, if you want. I don't have nothing to do."

"Me neither," Maureen said.

"You want to then?"

"I don't know. I suppose I shouldn't."

"That always makes it more fun."

"Does it?"

"You bet it does."

"Well, I lost my job today. The foreman lady yelled at me. I don't suppose I can get another one."

"Well, you oughta celebrate then. It isn't every day you're lucky enough to lose a job."

"I guess you're right."

Maureen was beginning to think Rosie wasn't nearly as bad as everybody said; in fact she was very nice.

But when they got to Rosie's cache, under the railroad trestle south of town, Maureen balked. Because it was an outdoor bedroom, partly roofed by the trestle, to keep it dry: old blankets, pillows, a sleeping bag, extra cigarettes, even cups for wine.

"I hate to drink out of the bottle," Rosie said. "It's not lady-like."

"Do you—sleep here sometimes?" Maureen said. She gestured toward the bedding on the matted ground.

Rosie, pouring wine, laughed so that her white teeth flashed in the brown face.

"Just long enough for you know what."

"I guess I know. It's what they all want, isn't it? My—well I mean I know because I'm like you, inside."

"I'm not sick, hell no."

"Not like that. Rotten, like garbage."

"Somebody's been trying to fuck your mind."

Maureen jumped. "I never heard a girl use a word like that before."

"Well, you have now. You gonna drink that wine, or just sit there and hold it?"

Maureen laughed: she felt *very* far from town. She took a big gulp of wine and discovered it was sweet and tasted like blackberries.

"This is wonderful wine. I love it."

"My boyfriend Henry bought it for me. Or stole it, more like."

"Can we smoke another Lucky with it?"

"Sure, I got a whole carton stashed. You can have anything you want, if you just know how to get it."

"Can you?" Maureen said. She tried to think about what she wanted. If she died, they would be sorry. Some people threw themselves off bridges. She looked up at the grey wooden beams rising dizzily. Maybe if you were drunk you could, it would be just like diving, the swift rush of air . . . .

"You want some more?"

Maureen nodded and held out the cup. "I don't care if I *do* get drunk. Nobody else cares, now, so why should I?"

"M hm," Rosie said, inhaling deeply, "you've got to look out for number one, that's what I always say. My boyfriend Alex has a friend you could meet."

"He wouldn't like me."

"That's what you think. He's got money, too—plenty of it."

Rosie filled Maureen's cup again. She felt dizzy now when she looked up into the maze of the bridge. She had never looked at a bridge from underneath before. Amazing how many timbers and planks it took, all crossed and re-crossed, just to let one little train go over. She wondered if the trainmen ever thought about that. It was as if those who had made the bridge had been scared that it would fall and had gone crazy, piling timber upon timber, so the whole thing wouldn't collapse.

"I just don't care," she told Rosie.

"Fuck no," Rosie said, "I don't care either." She took out another cigarette and studied it and then fixed Maureen with an unsteady eye. "Don't you try to steal any of my boyfriends, though—you hear?"

"I wouldn't do that," Maureen said. "I'm your friend. I'm your *best* friend."

Rosie waggled her head, frowning. "I've had best friends before—plenty of 'em."

When they started back along the roadbed, they hung on to each other's arms, to keep from falling over the ties. Maureen giggled.

"I was going to jump, but I guess I wasn't drunk enough," she said, gesturing toward the bridge behind them.

"That doesn't do you any good," Rosie said. "Nobody cares."

"They'd be sorry, though."

"That's what you think."

When they parted, Rosie suddenly turned on her. "You think you're such a fancy bitch everybody's going to give you everything for nothing, don't you?"

Maureen's face burned. "No, I don't. I just want to be friends, really."

"Huh! I know all about friends." And Rosie turned and marched unsteadily away up the sidewalk.

Maureen's shoulders slumped, watching. Rosie was angry at her too—they all hated her.

When she got to the house, her uncle was mowing the front lawn, walking ponderously, absorbed. Maureen threw herself on him without thinking.

"Uncle Bill, tell me what's wrong with me! Tell me what's *wrong*, I'm scared!"

But he pushed her away as if she had attacked him. He had been gone, mindless in the act of mowing the lawn, relaxing for once in his life, his consciousness a thousand miles away, and she had brought him back with a wrench. He smelled the wine immediately, and knew.

And all he could say was, "A sixteen-year-old girl—a sixteen-year-old girl—"

Because she stank with it, reeked of it. He knew he ought to take hold of her, to shake her, to tell her what she would do to all of them, what she would make the neighbors think. He knew he ought to whip her: drag her to the house and birch her good. He told himself he knew what was right and how to defend it. Yet in fact he only went red and raised his arms, helplessly, as if he would fend her off, protect himself from her. It was as if she had—as if her wild eyes, her breath, her tilting body—had unmanned him.

She was saying, "Nobody likes me and I lost my job and you said you wanted to help and I need it—"

And all he could say was, "Black coffee—you hear? Black coffee. Because even Christ had his limits—you hear me—even Christ!"

Then she was backing away from him as if he would truly strike her, staring at him wildly, turning quickly into the house.

Her aunt was in the kitchen, but Maureen didn't try to speak to her. She ran into her room, slammed the door, and threw herself on the bed, face down. In a moment she heard her aunt open the door.

"Now just what was *that* for, would you mind telling me?"

But Maureen couldn't answer. The bed tilted, the walls began to revolve, slowly. She held her breath to make it stop, and her aunt went away. In a moment Maureen knew she would be sick, and stumbled into the bathroom. After awhile she heard her aunt say, "Well, maybe your Uncle Bill was right about you, after all."

"I'm scared, Aunt Harriet."

"You ought to be scared. You'll bring up your whole insides, carrying on like that. I'd like to know who taught you to act like that. I truly would."

Afterward Maureen slept, fitfully, but she kept waking to find herself in midair, with the maze of the bridge beside her. She must have cried out, because her aunt was there holding her, stroking her forehead.

"There, there, sweetheart, it'll be all right—"

"You'd just as well save your pity till she sobers up, *I'd* say," her Uncle Bill said.

Then she was diving, but instead of water flowing around her it was blood; it was warm and when it entered her mouth, it tasted like blackberries.

She didn't get out of bed the next day. Wherever she turned her head, an image sprang up. She lay on the figured carpet; the tips of her fingers bristled with hairs; the empty pool opened, frost-hard, beside the bed, and she could hear the leaves rustling within it. She remembered they had a place to go, somewhere. When she closed her eyes, she swam in blood.

She was in the empty swimming pool and the leaves were razors, swirling around her. She had to get out and no one would help; they stood on the bridge above her, beyond the maze, and pierced her with their eyes. She had to think her way out, herself.

Maybe they all hated her because they all wanted it and she wouldn't give it—the women too, not for themselves but for the men. So maybe if she gave it to them, they wouldn't hate her anymore. They had hated her in Michigan because she hadn't given them what they wanted; it was true she hadn't because her mother had warned her, but maybe her mother hadn't really meant that. She had changed her mind about it since but she had wanted her to give it to him then, and because she wouldn't, they had hated her.

So now her aunt and uncle did, too. So maybe if she let them know she was willing, they would like her. It couldn't be much, anyway; Rosie did it every day and was healthy and strong and even proud. So it couldn't hurt her, if that's what they wanted. And they all wanted it: she knew that was true, herself.

Maureen got out of bed then and took off her bra and panties and put on the sheerest negligee she owned and stood in front of the mirror to make sure they could see everything. Then she stood a moment until her legs felt steady under her, and then went out into the living room where they were. She struck a pose, the way she had seen her mother do it, and tried her best to smile beckoningly at her Uncle Bill.

"Sweetheart—" her aunt said.

Maureen widened her smile for her, to let her know she was included too.

"*Now* what?" her uncle said. But she saw his face go pink under the lamplight, when he looked at her.

She walked to him, gliding her bare feet over the carpet, staring steadily at the hollow of his throat, smiling. She put her hand on his sleeve and slid it upward, scarcely touching him.

"Maureen, for God's sake—" and Maureen turned to smile at her aunt reassuringly.

Her Uncle Bill sat frozen, staring at the hand on his sleeve. He couldn't bring himself to look at her body again, thrust almost into his face.

"Maureen, honey, you're sick. You're fevered, your face is all flushed. Honey you don't know what you're doing—"

But the uncle had recovered. For an instant he had desired her, helplessly, and now he wanted to strike her, to cast her from him, because he knew it was not his niece who swayed her body toward him, who hooked her dark eyes into his; he knew who it was, and knew that he should strike him to the ground, cast him out into the howling wilderness, break his grip forever. And yet he thought: has he not come to bring me knowledge? How should I know my God without knowing his great enemy? What if I should touch her flesh—simply touch it? But he dared not, and only rose and stumbled away, as he had in the yard earlier, and raised his arm as if to defend himself.

"She's out of her mind, that's what she is. She tried to do this there and that's why they sent her away. You see what she is—look at her, look at her!"

"Bill, she's fevered, she's delirious—"

"She's burning with lust, that's what she is." He had backed away from Maureen and stood rigidly, pointing at her, not daring to look at her. "And if you let her stay she'll contaminate us all—I warn you—"

"Bill, she's a child—"

"She's old, Harriet. I tell you she's older than any of us—"

"It's all right," Maureen said. "I don't feel bad about it any more. Mama warned me, so I was afraid of it, the way they looked at me. But I understand now. You never looked at me like that. And I know it isn't so bad now, really I do. I won't tell anybody, either, I promise."

"You get her out of here," her uncle said.

"You don't want me? It's all right, honest it is—"

"Get her out, Harriet—now!"

Then her aunt had her arms around her bare shoulder, hugging her. And her aunt was afraid: something about the child's glance, her smile. She did not believe for a minute in the child as temptress. She was ill, and in her delirium had tried to act out some scene she only half understood. Mrs. Ord didn't care where it came from. Let sleeping dogs lie. Her duty was to get the child well again.

She led Maureen back into her bedroom.

"But I want you to like me. I don't care about the other thing."

"Sweetheart we *love* you. You don't have to do anything. You're delirious, and tomorrow when the fever's gone it'll all seem like a bad dream. You have to go to bed now, and sleep."

"Uncle Bill doesn't like me."

"Sweetheart you startled him. You upset him. He didn't know how to react, that's all. He didn't realize how sick you are, that's all."

"Please don't turn out the light, will you?"

"I promise I won't until you're sound asleep. And tomorrow if you're not better, I'll call the doctor."

She tucked the covers in around Maureen, her hands very gentle.

"You want some warm milk, honey? To help you sleep?"

"No."

When she had gone it was as if warm water had flowed through a drain, and Maureen was in the dry pool again with the leaves.

She closed her eyes and forced herself to breath regularly, and after awhile she heard her aunt tiptoe in and turn out the light. Then Maureen listened until she heard them go into their bedroom, arguing sharply in whispers. Then she got up and went to the bathroom and shut the door. She took a deep breath, to steady herself. Her mind felt clear as water: she was happy, her limbs buoyant and quick. Enough light shone through the window from the street for her to see what she needed. She found one almost immediately on the shelf, peeled away its paper cover and held it a moment in the light, to watch it flash. Then she gripped it firmly and drew it deeply across her left wrist.

She was surprised that there should be so much, though it didn't scare her. But the surprise made her sit down on the toilet and put her mouth over the wound, instinctively. And it was warm and sweet, as she had known it would be. She felt a little dizzy, suddenly, and very contented, as if a great pressure had been released.

But she had forgotten to lock the door, and her aunt had either heard her or sensed that she had got up. Because now she suddenly opened the door and snapped on the light.

"Oh sweet Jesus protect us—"

Then she screamed.

## II

They took her to their own doctor and because he had a mustache, Maureen couldn't talk, so he gave them the name of a psychiatrist who told her she hadn't really wanted to kill herself, she had only wanted attention, like a little child, and then she couldn't talk to him, either, and sat staring at him or maybe at nothing and kneading her hands, so he recommended they commit her to the state hospital.

*Kill myself*, she was thinking: what a strange idea. If she had wanted to do that, she would have got drunk and jumped off the railroad bridge.

The Ords felt very strange, being in a psychiatrist's office, and wondering whether anyone they knew might have seen them entering there. They felt even stranger about having to commit their niece to an insane asylum. ("Can it really be that serious, Bill?

96

Because it seems so *sudden*, the poor little thing.") So Harriet called
Stella who was in Reno by then, but Stella sounded vague, over the
phone, as if she were drugged or half asleep.

"If you think it's the best, Harriet—" It was almost as if she had
been glad to hear it because maybe now she thought Maureen
couldn't accuse her any more, or was so stunned at whatever she
herself had done to her or allowed to happen to her that she couldn't
even conceive clearly what was happening. In any case there was
no depending on Stella: whatever they did they would have to do
on their own.

So they called the state hospital and made an appointment for
that same afternoon.

Driving north through the afternoon heat Harriet kept staring
off into nowhere, because it had all spun out of control so fast. Bill
remembered how he had felt about his own niece, naked under her
negligee, and gripped the steering wheel as if he would break it.

Maureen sat between them (they were afraid to leave her in the
back seat alone) and watched the fields and smelled the ripening
grapes, their odor carried hot into the open side window of the car.
Ever since she had done it, she had felt calm, her mind as smooth
as a still pond. And happy: she caught herself smiling for no reason
at all. And she had scarcely seen the images: it was as if she had
drained the foulness out of herself.

The Ords were surprised at how young the head doctor was—
and handsome, in a dark Italian way, with a beard so dense his
shaven jaw looked blue. Dr. Lolas.

But he talked very slowly and calmly, and looked them both in
the eye, so that they were soon reassured. Yes, it certainly appeared
that their niece ought to stay for two or three days, he said, to let him
see what the trouble might be, before they did anything official.
These things took time. Perhaps it wouldn't be necessary to do
anything at all, by way of treatment. Adolescence was a hard time
for anybody. Perhaps just a few days' rest—

Maureen loved his voice, the way it flowed over her. She sat in
a leather chair and felt laved by Dr. Lolas' voice. Nothing bad could
happen to you while that voice sounded. She felt it.

She had to say good-bye to her aunt and uncle in the reception
room, because no visitors were allowed on the wards. The nurse
who questioned her for admission kept staring up at her suspi-
ciously; then Maureen noticed the white walls, the worn tile floor,

97

the barred windows, a philodendron tied to a rusty curtain rod, its head drooping above where the string cut into it. She stared at her little overnight bag, that didn't even have a swimming suit in it. A bored male attendant stood to one side, waiting to take her to the ward where she would sleep. She had thought Dr. Lolas would be there himself, to take her. He had seemed to care so much. But he didn't reappear. The nurse went on with her questions relentlessly. Maureen's aunt answered most of them. Her Uncle Bill paced as if he were caged.

Though she was only being admitted for observation her aunt and uncle had to sign the forms. Then Maureen suddenly knew, watching the pen move, that it had all been a mistake. She couldn't let them go, she didn't belong here, she didn't know anybody, she was frightened.

"Sweetheart, it's only for a couple of days. They want to *help* you. We don't know what to do, don't you see, because we're not doctors. But that nice young Dr. Lolas will know. And we'll call you every day and in two or three days we can come back and take you home again and everything will be all right—"

"*Please* don't leave me here. I'm scared, I don't know anybody—"

"Sweetheart we *have* to. We don't know what else to do. You have to get well, don't you see? So you don't hurt yourself any more."

"But I feel good now, I'm not sick anymore, I scarcely ever see them, even, it's true—"

"Oh, sweetheart." Her aunt held her then, her clean-smelling body enfolded her. But they would go, anyway.

Her Uncle Bill stood off to one side, mute, looking half-sick to his stomach. He didn't even want to look at her, as if he knew they were abandoning her, really, now, that they had pretended to want her and now admitted it was a lie. Except that maybe he had wanted her the other way, and had recoiled from her because of it.

She was still looking at them as they crossed the parking lot. When they got the car turned around, she was nowhere to be seen. They drove all the way home in the heat without finding a single thing to say to each other. Sometimes on hot days the heat increased after dark. This was one of those days.

# III

They didn't come back in three days or in four, and her aunt called her only twice in the first week, and then there was nothing to say.

Mostly she sat on the ward and listened to the radio or walked around the lawns among the attendants and the other patients. Dr. Lolas came to talk to her the second day and asked her questions about her mother and father. She couldn't answer the ones about her father because she scarcely even remembered what he looked like; Dr. Lolas apparently did not know that Maureen had only seen her father two or three times since she was four, and she never bothered to inform him. So she simply didn't know whether he had ever done anything to frighten her, or if she had ever seen him do anything to frighten her mother, or if she had ever seen him naked, or seen him and her mother make love. She couldn't answer the questions about her mother because they were all about how she *felt* about her, and she didn't know. She couldn't tell him about Eliot and Michigan because she had sworn to herself never to tell anyone, and after Michigan she could almost never think about her mother; even when she read her letters, the sentences blurred in her mind. So she didn't know whether she loved her, and said yes automatically, and didn't know whether she was jealous of her because she couldn't even imagine what that might mean, and said no. But Dr. Lolas accepted everything she said calmly: there were apparently no wrong answers. He seemed very interested when he had asked her to describe her mother and she had said she was very beautiful. But he never smiled, and Maureen liked that. He had dark brown eyes and looked at you seriously all the time, and his voice flowed over you, soothingly. Somehow he would help her, she knew he would.

Then he disappeared for several days. Maureen questioned the ward nurses, and they told her he would be back to see her, of course, but he hadn't said when. He was a very busy man. Maureen wasn't the only patient in this hospital by any means: there were some very sick people here. It was true, of course, she *wasn't* really sick—they left the lights on at the ends of the ward at night, so she had scarcely seen any of the images at all and because of the pills they gave her, she dropped off to sleep like a stone; still she felt a little hurt at being told to her face that she hadn't any right to want to see Dr. Lolas when there were so many who really needed him.

The lady in the next bed played hearts with her when she wasn't too sleepy from the pills and then taught her to play rummy, which made the time pass. Her name was Mrs. Daley, and she said she was a schizophrenic, which didn't mean anything to Maureen because she acted like everyone else she had ever known. All the people at the hospital did, except for a couple. Mrs. Daley brushed her hair and told her how pretty she was and gave her cigarettes until Maureen felt guilty and went down to the commissary store and bought a package of Luckies so she could pay her back. That was one thing about being here: you could smoke all you liked and no one ever told you not to.

She didn't mind being in the hospital, really; mostly the patients were nice and left you alone, and it was a relief not to feel her aunt and uncle wondering about her, worrying. And except for the questions Dr. Lolas had asked her she thought even less about her mother here than she had at her aunt's. Only she wished there was a swimming pool.

A young intern talked to her occasionally, without seeming very interested. He would look at her chart and ask her how she was feeling and did she need anything, and then nod and look uncomfortable for a moment and then move on. She was in for observation, but nobody seemed to be doing any observing. She told her aunt this, once, when she called, but she told her to be patient because surely they knew what was best for her.

Then Dr. Lolas started to visit her every day, sometimes twice a day. He would sit down beside her and offer her a cigarette and ask her to talk about whatever she liked. And if Maureen wasn't too sleepy, she would tell him about swimming and Josh White and Harry Belafonte and a horse she had loved, once when she and her mother had lived on a ranch briefly. Then he would tell her about growing up in New York, and describe the complicated rules of the sidewalk games they played, and tell her how you knew everybody in your neighborhood there, but that it was very hard to get to know anybody really.

Once he asked her if she was a loner and when Maureen nodded, he told her he was too, so they were two of a kind, really. Then she felt very proud, that she should be like someone who was as smart and as wise as Dr. Lolas was. She didn't understand why he talked to her every day about such ordinary, unimportant things, but she supposed maybe that was what observation was all about. She had never talked much, with anybody, so it was just nice that somebody wanted to.

Then one Friday Dr. Lolas announced that he had a swimming pool at his ranch, and if Maureen was a very, very good girl, he would see that she got a pass for the weekend so she could come and swim all she liked. It was the closest she had ever seen him come to smiling. Maureen hadn't had her morning pill yet and so tingled all over with anticipation and could only nod. The hospital would be like a wonderful summer camp, finally—not the prison she had feared when her aunt had left her here.

Dr. Lolas made good his word: an attendant came to wake Maureen in the afternoon and led her down to the main reception room so she could sign the form for the pass, and Dr. Lolas' neat signature was already there, below where hers would go. The attendant and the nurse behind the desk exchanged a look which Maureen didn't understand. She could already feel the water moving along her slick sides, the vibration of the board in the soles of her feet, humming.

Dr. Lolas talked constantly, on the drive to the ranch, describing the landscape and the trees and the crops—it was all so new to him, after New York. He smoked constantly, too, and half the time he forgot to offer Maureen one. He was talking so much he missed the turn to the ranch, and had to drive on for a quarter of a mile and turn around and come back. Then he did smile, for the first time, as if he were laughing at himself.

As soon as they got to the house she asked him where it was, and he took her to it without a word, as if he sensed that until she saw it, nothing else would matter to her, nothing else would really exist, not even himself.

The sun burned low over the hills, and heat waves blurred the trees beyond the yard. Maureen stood on the edge beside the diving board and watched the water move along the green tile. She had been sleepy in the car from the morning pill, but now she felt the tingling in her legs again. Before she had scarcely let herself think about it and now it lay so close she could lift her foot and touch it and it belonged to her, the whole shining length of it, for hours— days even.

"Will you swim too?" She didn't want to share it with anybody.

Dr. Lolas shook his head, almost smiling again. "I've some

101

homework to do. But I'll sit here and be your lifeguard."

She watched him set his briefcase down on the cement and take off his suit coat and throw it over the back of a lawn chair and loosen his tie. He scarcely existed for her, the pool drew her so powerfully; he was kind but she wished he would go away. But he was nodding at her, still almost smiling, as if he knew what she was feeling, and approved.

"You want a Coke?"

She shook her head and he went into the house. In a moment he came back with a cigarette in one hand and a tall clinking cocktail glass in the other and sat down in the lawn chair. He set the glass down and put the cigarette in his mouth, opened the briefcase and took out a clipboard and a couple of manila folders with papers in them. Then he looked up at her.

"You O.K., are you? Not feeling woozy from the medication?"

Maureen shook her head.

"You want a smoke first?"

She shook her head again: every movement, every word was agony for her.

Then she made herself say, "I don't even have a suit."

He waved his cigarette indifferently, arranging the papers. "Doesn't matter. I'm a doctor, remember? And nobody else will bother us, I promise." He looked at her. "I'll defend you against all comers."

She thought about asking him to turn his back, but he seemed busy with the papers, and besides he had probably already looked at her a dozen times while she was sleeping. All the women on the ward went to sleep drugged, so they never know if a doctor or an attendant or anyone who felt like it, had looked at them in the night.

She undid the buttons at the back of her frock, then pulled it over her head. She thought for a moment about leaving her bra and panties on, but they would be wet still in the morning, and besides he was a doctor, so it didn't matter anyway, did it?

Still when she began lapping the pool, she stole glances at him to see if he was watching her, but he seemed absorbed in his work except once when she stopped at the far end of the pool for a moment, he saluted her with his glass and nodded approvingly.

Then she forgot him completely and let the rhythm of the swimming take her. At first she could not, though, because the drugs had made her muscles slack. When she tried to force them to move well, she found herself chopping at the water, twisting and flailing. She made herself stop trying then and floated on her back with her eyes closed until she knew she wouldn't try to force it again. Then when she began swimming, the rhythm came, and she let herself sink into it so deeply that everything but the water and her own motion disappeared.

She came to supper with red eyes and wrinkled palms, utterly contented. She loved Dr. Lolas, for having given her the best thing of all.

Then she saw the pill lying beside her glass of milk. She picked it up and showed it to him, where he stood by the stove filling their plates.

"Do I have to, even here?"

He nodded. "It's important."

"But it—makes it hard to swim."

"Well, maybe you can skip it in the morning, then. But you better go ahead and take it tonight, so you'll sleep. It takes awhile to build the level up, so if you stop, they're not as effective for a day or two."

"Why do I need them, anyway?"

"To keep you calm."

"Will I always need them then?"

"Well, some people do, but when you're really rested, you'll probably feel better about yourself, and then you'll only need them now and again when you're under stress."

"What's that—stress?"

"Oh, you know, when you're anxious about meeting somebody, or starting a new job or a new school—that sort of thing."

When he set their steaming plates on the table—canned beef stew and green peas, with a slice of buttered bread beside it— Maureen suddenly realized she was so hungry she would have to force herself to eat slowly. Absorbed in the smell of the food, she took the pill with a gulp of milk, almost without realizing.

After supper Dr. Lolas went on with his paper work and seemed content to ignore her. She asked him if she could sample his records, and he told her of course; so she sat in front of the fat warm walnut cabinet and took out the albums, playing parts of them she knew, sometimes three or four times over. Before nine o'clock she was getting very sleepy. Dr. Lolas showed her where she would sleep and turned back the covers on the bed. It was the largest bed she had ever seen, so immense that she would have laughed, if she hadn't been so sleepy. She took off her clothes and stretched out: she could have lain sideways and still not touched the sides.

In a moment Dr. Lolas reappeared, in slippers and a bathrobe. He sat down on the edge of the bed and put his hand on her throat and the side of her face as if testing for fever.

But he looked at her very seriously and said, "Have you ever made love with anyone before?"

Maureen shook her head. She felt so warm and sleepy in the enormous bed that she wasn't at all surprised to hear him ask that: it was as though she had expected it.

"Well it's very, very good for you, especially if you feel bad about yourself sometimes, like you do, and especially if you have someone who really knows how to be gentle with you. You understand?"

Maureen nodded, smiling up at him encouragingly. She felt happy that she could give him what he wanted, because he was so nice to her. She could lie and let his voice flow over her forever.

"You want to then? Because it would only be good for you if you really wanted to."

Maureen nodded again and Dr. Lolas let out a sigh as if he had been holding his breath.

He got up then and turned out the light, and in a moment she felt his body touch hers and cringed a little, because it was covered with hair.

Dr. Lolas stroked her and kissed her a long time on the mouth. She loved kissing him, except for the roughness of his close-shaved beard. After awhile he put his hand on her thighs and eased them apart. But when he touched her maidenhead, he muttered "Damn," and went slack for a moment, as if he were exhausted. Then he recovered, turned in the bed and thrust his face where his hand had been. She felt his tongue probing her and arched to receive him. He fumbled for her hand and put it on him and showed her how to stroke him there.

When he had shuddered and fallen away from her, he lay as if dead. As for Maureen, the tingling she had felt in her legs, earlier, now ran all through her body: she had never felt better in her life.

Dr. Lolas got up and put his robe and slippers on and lit a cigarette. Maureen could scarcely keep her eyes open now, but she suddenly realized the doctor was tense—angry perhaps. She had wanted to please him more than anything, but somehow she had failed: she could see it in the way he smoked.

Finally he said, "Are you all right?" He had tried to make his voice gentle, but Maureen could feel the other thing, disappointment or maybe even hatred. She had failed him somehow, and he hated her for it. He sat on the bed, tense, and smoked.

"You're not sorry?"

She shook her head but she knew there was nothing she could do about the way he was feeling.

He patted the covers over her leg and said, "You're a good girl," but she could hear it in his voice, unmistakable, and that was the last thing she remembered.

When she got back on the ward Sunday afternoon, Mrs. Daley asked her how her visit with the doctor had gone, and when Maureen told her he had slept with her, Mrs. Daley surprised her by saying, "Why the dirty bastard. But nobody would ever dare accuse him, would they? The dirty son of a bitch."

The pills must have been working or else the doctors and nurses had observed all they needed to because before the week was out, they told Maureen her aunt and uncle were coming to take her home. She put on her best white blouse and green skirt to meet them, but she remembered Mrs. Daley's reaction and didn't tell them about Dr. Lolas—not even about the pool. She was never to tell anybody about it for a long, long time.


**W. C. Keep**: This is the second chapter from a novel also entitled *The Swimmer*. The story continues with Maureen's nightmare episodes in other madhouses. Then she tries for awhile to cling to a man who cares for her but who cannot reach or even understand her deep, distorted self. In the end we see her, not quite alone, beginning to make her way out of the woods and into the light.

I write and teach English in Bellingham, Washington. Previously, my work has been published in *Carleton Miscellany*, *Poetry Northwest*, and *Prairie Schooner*.

# Psychiatrist/God

God sat there at the head of the couch, with his pad and his gold Cross pen, and just as I took no comfort from the concept of a God, I was able to take no comfort from him. He was judge and jury and I feared him much as I feared the theistic God.

"Why didn't you tell anyone?" he asked again.

I had previously answered that question in as many ways as I could think of—I didn't know—my mother wouldn't have believed me—I feared punishment. But, God wasn't satisfied, I was failing his test. I tried again.

"I liked it," remembering the toys, the candy, the hugs no one else got.

The pen scratched furiously. "Bingo," I thought and God's silent but audible "AHA!" fell on me like a steel gavel, sentencing me to a newer, fresher, more clear-cut guilt. If I liked it, then I had been the aggressor, the perpetrator, the instigator, the source of all the evil. The ludicrous image of a four-year-old child sexually seducing, encouraging, molesting a sixty-year-old grandfather never entered my head. I was guilty as charged.

\* \* \* \*

This is a version (excerpted from my journal) of an analytic session with a psychiatrist I saw in the early 1960s. The treatment was largely unsuccessful, and I left a year later feeling more futile than before. In retrospect, I suspect he was dealing with a problem about which he had little information and not much experience.

Norma Rothstein

# The Lie

You said letting you make love to me
would make me a woman
I was only 11 and desperately wanted
to be grown-up

Now I am 32 and feel like a child trapped
in a woman's body
Somehow, after you were through with me
I quit growing
It was all I could do to survive


**Judy DeVries:** It took twenty years, two daughters and a shaky marriage before I could write "The Lie." It took another year to show it to a counselor and say "help." Submitting it to *Rebirth of Power* was another step toward healing—just as not using a pseudonym is.

I am still in therapy, my marriage is still shaky and there is much pain in dealing with the past. However, I have something I didn't have before—HOPE.

# I am a Woman

I am a woman whose life is a river
parted down the middle for Pharoah's army
to plunge in; drown. The scream of the
horse echoes in my bloody womb, slit
like the wrist of the western sky.

I am a woman whose life is a temple,
a stable of gods & fragments of lost poems
torn from a mysterious yesterday. Whose
altar holds the heart, holds the fragile
beating, an offering for Diana.

I am a woman whose life is a thread
stretched taut across death, a silent
bridge broken by the emergency of being
born. Incense spirals thru stone circles,
spins into the attic of my childhood.

The web shivers and I know.
I know, I know.

**Beth-Luis-Nion:** When I wrote "I am a Woman," I had no conscious memory of being raped as a child. Now I understand how my deep inner wisdom was telling my molest experiences symbolically until I had a support system where it was safe to remember. Writing has been a survival tool. It still is.

# Old Woman in the Woods: An Incest Fable

Once upon a time there was a young girl with lots of black curls on her head and dragon-green eyes. She was a small child—so small she often disappeared—poof—into nowhere. One minute she'd be in a room full of grown-ups, dancing, saying clever things, showing off. The grown-ups would admire her, pat her head, kiss her and hug her. Then, suddenly, she wasn't there anymore. The grown-ups would talk to each other about grown-up things, and, although the girl was sure she was standing in exactly the same place she had been before, she was invisible. All those grown-ups who had loved and cared about her, seemingly so much, were no longer there. She was confused. She pinched herself, then cut herself—just to see her blood, just to be sure she was real.

* * * *

The old woman sat in the woods one sunny Springtime day— watching for a rabbit or a deer. She listened to the birds, she listened for some word of her lost childhood. The dreams. If only she could recapture last night's dream—the words about the Night. The Night. The Lost Childhood. The Eyes In The Closet. Her father. What had she ever wanted from him in all those fifty-odd years she knew him before he died? Only for him to love her.

* * * *

He wasn't a nice man, her father. He was ever so respected. A businessman. President of this civic club and that one. But her father was not a nice man. Those Eyes In The Closet—always watching her. The old woman shivers in the sunlight.

Her father is standing there, saying "ohmigod." He looks at the girl. He is holding his Thing in his hand. White oosh squirts out of it. The girl is frightened. How big is she? How old is she? Is she even smaller than five? Does he spill it on her? In his own hand? Does he flee into the bathroom? The old woman does not remember. She licks her lips. They are salty. Is that only the taste of sweat? Or is it remembered semen? Why won't this wetness between her legs go away?

She remembers the girl. Night after night of pre-pubescent masturbation. Desperate. Frantic. Always frantic. Like most of her adult sex life. Frantic. How often did she find satisfaction—or was it only exhaustion?

That little girl with dark curls and green eyes haunts the old woman. Now Daddy is teaching the little girl to dance. She is so small that she stands on the tip of his shoes while he dances around the room. The Eyes In The Closet watch them. Her head touches his belt buckle. Her father reaches down and adjusts his pants. He presses the child's face on the fat stick he keeps inside his trousers. He unbuckles his belt and opens his fly. She stares at his pee-pee. "Daddy wants to show you something," he says, taking his penis into his hands. Lifting it out of his trousers. Touching it to her lips. Brushing it back and forth against the child's mouth. "See. It's just like an ice cream cone. Let's see you lick it. You can make believe it's an ice cream cone."

* * * *

In the forest, the old woman stretches out on a bed of last winter's oak leaves. Her hands move downward to her own moist warmth between her legs. She wishes it would go away. She wishes it would never happen. She slips her hands beneath her Levi's, her fingers touch her clitoris. She brings herself to climax.

She gets up, walks to a sun-filled meadow, takes off her shirt, her shoes, her sox. She sleeps. Everywhere, on all sides, the birds are singing.

Her burden has become lighter. Her breasts, soft, against the tenderness of the Great Mother. Her thoughts droning a prayer, "Take my pain, Mother. Cleanse me. Heal me with your Spring-time."

110

**Marylou Hadditt:** I am 59 years old, a strong feminist, and a recent lesbian. The incest surfaced only six years ago, after half a lifetime of repression. Writing has been my salvation—not writing for publication but writing for myself—journal entries, fairy tales, unmailed letters . . . I can only speculate about how the abuse affected my marriage, profession, and motherhood. Today, my adult children are supportive of me . . . even now, as I write, I feel an enormous sadness. Someday, I will leave it behind me.

# The Magic Wolf

*Send your spirit into an animal; call it back again.*
—Salish Indian song

As a child at night I would imagine the wolves racing under a hunter's moon, the pack in full cry. Their voices fell like silver, a quavering in the throat at first, then the power of the chorus gaining strength until the sound seemed to stroke my spine and raise every hair on my body.

I would sit up in bed in my darkened room as if I expected them to appear on our suburban front lawn, a circle of wolves in the moonlight. As if I expected them to come for me. *Yes.* I pulled up my knees and buried my face against them, willing with all my strength for those wild creatures to appear. *Yes.* Even though I knew they would never come.

I had turned eleven that year. In recent months, my father had started acting strangely toward me. My sister, my brother, and I had always felt both love and hate for him. He could be funny and playful at times, but he was also a harsh, authoritarian man whose punishments were swift and often brutal. We could never really relax around him, and at times we wished he would go off somewhere and never come back. Lately he had been saying things that frightened and angered me.

"I want you to look after my clothes and fold my underwear and put it in my drawer. You should learn to take care of a man, anticipate his needs. It will be good training for you as a wife."

I was confused. Shouldn't my mother be doing that for him? She worked full time in a dental office, and I had taken over many of her household jobs. I often cooked dinner for the five of us; my brother and sister filled in other chores. I made sure the laundry was done and that my sister did her homework. I had been doing these things since I was nine years old, but my father had never talked to me this way.

"Men are brutes," he would say. "They only want one thing, and when they're through, they leave. The woman gets stuck with the booby prize, and the man gets off scot free. When it happens to

112

you, bring it on home. Don't take it somewhere else."

Why is he telling me this? I wondered. What does it mean, that I'm bad?

Now when he hugged me, he told me to spread my legs farther apart and would press his body too tightly into mine. I didn't know why I disliked it so much, but part of me felt I must be doing something to make this happen. He *wanted* so much from me; I could feel it in his body. Whenever we were alone in the car or at home he would talk about sex or tell dirty jokes. It made me feel as if I were sharing in some smutty secret.

I thought my mother must know how to handle this. Mastering my embarrassment about bringing up the subject, I asked her, "Why does Dad talk about sex so much? Every time we go anywhere, it always comes up. I don't like it."

She shrugged, stirring the soup on the stove. "Well, that's the way men are," she said vaguely.

Her tone of voice made my heart sink: *That's the way men are and there's nothing we can do about it.* I didn't mention the subject again.

Not long after that my father started coming into my bedroom at night and lying beside me. I remembered little of what happened. When he left, the smell of his body clung to the sheets and to my skin. Often during those nights he would murmur, "Some fathers go to jail for raping their daughters. But I have control."

His words frightened me. What if his control slipped? What would happen to me then?

I turned to the only ally I knew and sent my spirit into the wolf to keep it safe. Sometimes, when my father was on top of me or unbuttoning my blouse to stroke my breasts, I saw a white wolf racing after a stag that had once been a man. The wolf, like a ghost, leapt on the stag and brought it down. I felt the swift, savage click of powerful jaws close on my father's throat and the blood flowed warm like madness. The clean kill. Not like the murder I felt taking root in my heart. The wolf had no blame and no guilt.

I had always loved wild animals. Their spirit, unfettered by our human will, seemed part of the mystery I touched when walking alone in the country. As children, my sister and I felt drawn to the life we sensed in the open fields and gullies that surrounded our small suburban town then. We learned to mimic animal voices. We could howl like wolves and set every dog in the neighborhood barking. We learned to hide in the brush like foxes, to cultivate the

113

alertness of our cat. We drank from our cupped hands and lay on one side with our arms stretched out like forelegs. We created a world our father couldn't enter.

I read stories about wolves and collected pictures of them that I kept hidden away in a book. I would look at them late at night with a flashlight under the covers and dream about being with them, far away from this place. I loved the long, fluid line of their bodies and the powerful muscles that drove them tirelessly, mile after mile. When I was older, I promised myself, I would set out for the wilderness and I would find them, the great white wolves of the Canadian forests, and I would live with them.

I did not want to be human, did not want to be growing into a woman. I prayed each night I would wake up changed into a boy or an animal. Maybe then my father would leave me alone. I developed a terror of the dark and the truth I might find there—my true human face. Not a wolf's body but something alien and hideous.

Like a totem animal, the wolf came and stayed with me. I could escape into its magic and shut out my father's hands on my body. I felt I had a secret power he could not touch, that I could use to protect my sister and my mother from the knowledge of what was happening. The family must not split up, even though my father talked about divorce. He and my mother fought often then, usually over us. I believed somehow that as long as I gave him a little of what he wanted, he would not leave.

My mother noticed there was a struggle going on between my father and me, and it worried her. She would take me aside every now and then and talk about how much my father loved me.

"Try to show him more affection," my mother would say. "He needs to know you care about him."

My heart ached for her. She seemed so innocent to me, concerned only with fixing what she thought was wrong. How could I tell her?

The scream I never uttered turned into a long, sobbing wail within me, a howl that floated across the land frozen in a perpetual winter inside. There were times when I seemed to have no feelings. Only when I slipped into that animal self did I feel alive.

I entered high school and, with the exception of one or two friends, kept away from most people. The idea of dating filled me with terror—I was sure the boys would be like my father. When-

114

ever I could slip away, I took long walks in the countryside, trying to leave the pain behind me, walking until I could breathe again and the old tightness in my chest was gone. My feet stroked the rich, black earth. Some evenings the sun threw its color high in the west and touched everything, even my skin, with a soft, golden light. A clear, arching sky cleaved the loneliness from me, and I felt no separation anywhere. The animals I saw seemed to accept me as one of them. Sometimes I would throw my head back and close my eyes and feel a fierce, aching joy for my life.

When I came home from those long walks, often in the dark, I caught sight of my mother in the lighted kitchen window. She seemed so good to me then; she represented all that was civilized and fragile, all that kept me tied to the human world. And here I was bringing into her home a daughter who was only partly human, a wild creature that cared nothing for our family order and stitched homilies and her hopes for grandchildren. I could not care about school activities, either, or the dances or the things she had done as a girl. All of it seemed so remote, meant for other people who belonged here. I felt that someday my real parents would come for me and explain my exile to this country.

All my instincts were wrong for being with people. At a church youth group meeting, I spent the time staring out the window at the birds flying north. I had a hard time concentrating in school and often felt nauseated without knowing why. I envied the easy way my friends could talk and hug each other. I didn't like being touched and was afraid to wrestle with any of my friends because it triggered the animal response *attack!* Sometimes I turned away from them in tears, not knowing what was wrong with me. Maybe I was a throwback to some more primitive race.

I stopped bringing my girlfriends home because my father could not keep his hands off them. We even discovered that he had spied on two of us in the shower. Ashamed, I tried to see my friends at their houses as much as possible.

When I conquered my fear enough to date a boy or go to a party, the setting seemed all wrong. I had the ridiculous desire to go off into the darkness with the boy—not to make out, but to race across the open fields like two wild animals hunting. Something pulled me toward the open windows rather than the brightly lighted room and the people laughing and dancing there. I felt as if I were searching for my own kind and was afraid they did not exist.

115

My father seemed both relieved and jealous when I started dating. He told me, "I'll be envious of the man that has intercourse with you."

I hated the thought of him imagining me having sex with any boy, as if nothing I could do would be private. After a time, I stopped dating.

The wolf stayed with me all through high school, my silent, invisible shaman. It taught me cunning, how to hide the truest part of myself so that no adult could find it. I let only one or two friends get close to me, and even they did not know about me and my father. When anyone came too near, the wolf was up in a flash, teeth bared, until I told it to lie down. Its wisdom seemed to speak of the inner spirit, pointing away from the world I had been born into toward another world with a different language and different gods. I found some of that language in Indian songs and legends telling of animal powers shared by humans or given to those who sought them. I needed to know so much, and there was no one to teach me. I tried talking to the minister at our church, but the words wouldn't come, and after a time I gave up going to church altogether.

The incest stopped before I left home for college. I carried the two worlds with me all through my years at the university. I achieved top scholastic honors, which made my parents happy. But a darkness seemed to be growing inside that I could not change. I felt I could imitate some of the emotions of being human, but I did not feel them. In fact, much of the time I was among people, I felt nothing at all.

Yet I could not forget that I was human; as much as I might hate it, I had a woman's body. Neither could I forget that my power came from my magical wolf. It was the only thing inside me that felt clean. All the rest seemed cowardly and corrupted. The human part of me was afraid of everything—of the dark, of being attacked, of the terrible emptiness within.

I left college after obtaining a master's degree. I married and then divorced after three years. I began a career as an editor and dreamed of writing short stories or novels one day. I met a man I liked, and we started dating. In every way I knew, I tried to build a normal life.

But the old split would not heal. Every spring and fall, when the sun traveled further north or south, that wild spirit within paced frantically to get away. Everything seemed to tell me: *Leave this place.* The wolf tugged at me, whining in its eagerness. My head was filled with images of wild beaches and marshlands, the sun warm on the sand and the salt air filling my lungs. Or I would see northern mountains with pines like spires and lakes set in the jeweled circles of extinct volcanoes. Yet I couldn't leave; I couldn't follow the migration, knowing if I did, I would lose what little of my human self I had left. The wolf, puzzled but loyal, stayed behind. A persistent fear of dying began to haunt me.

By the time I was in my mid-thirties, I could no longer keep thoughts of suicide out. I had left my job as an editor to be a free-lance writer, which meant I spent less time with people and worked at home. I was now living with the man I had found, but I was having more and more trouble being able to go out of the apartment. The fear seemed to pervade the very air I breathed, and I kept waiting for the attack I was sure would come. At times I would find myself half running home from the train until I was safe in my apartment again. I could not feel any connections with people. We would talk, but nothing seemed to be exchanged, as though we had simply signed to each other in passing. The world began to feel more and more hostile to me.

Yet from the outside, everything appeared to be going so well. I was successful in my career, had a good relationship, and kept up with my family despite the fact it was often hard to be with them. I could not understand why I felt I wasn't making it, as if I were sliding inexorably down a black hole. Had I cut off my life source by choosing my human side? Was I getting ready to die?

The paranoia became so bad I finally went to see a therapist. By now I could not talk with anyone more than a few minutes without a sense of panic rising up that shut off conversation. The therapist, a young woman in her thirties with short blonde hair and a kind face, asked me to describe how I experienced a typical day. After I had finished, she asked, "Have you ever been attacked by anyone?"

I shook my head. Her next question caught me by surprise.

"Do you identify with any animal?"

"Yes! A wolf. I've always felt a kinship with wolves. Why?"

"Very often people with paranoid structures will identify closely with an animal. Tell me something about your family. How many of you were there? What were your father and mother like?"

I described the five of us, the image we had in our neighbor-

117

hood of being the ideal family group, how we had become the local overachievers. The therapist listened closely, then asked, "What kind of relationship did you have with your father?"

I hesitated, then mentioned as clinically and briefly as I could that he had made sexual advances to me.

"Did your mother know?"

"No! She was away at work all the time."

"Let me just say that we've found in such families the mother often knows something is going on. Why don't we explore that a little next time?"

I left the session upset and frightened. That night I had a terrible nightmare. I was in a three-story house, and it was dark, except for a strange, yellowish light in one corner of the first floor hallway. While I was frantically looking for something in one room after the other, I felt the yellow light like an evil, malignant presence stalking me throughout the house. I woke up, crying in terror, and huddled against the wall until daylight.

That morning I canceled my next session with the therapist and dropped therapy altogether. My problem, I decided, was simply a lack of self-esteem, and that was a matter of the will. The animal part of me had to be integrated, that was all. It was clearly a case of letting my imagination run away with me.

For the next three years I tried meditation, self-help courses, guided imagery, creativity workshops, yoga, the art of self-defense, Jungian analysis, and Sufism. I buried myself in free-lance projects, joined a church, and worked for the liberation of South Africa, Korea, the Philippines, and Central America. I'm sure if there had been oppression on the dark side of the moon, I would have fought against that as well.

Each time I would get a little fix of self-esteem, then it would fade. The fear did not go away; I felt no more human than I ever had. All it took was the wind scuttling leaves on a late fall evening, the light as it fell over the city at sunset, or the sight of a crescent moon, and the old ache to go "home" would come back. I didn't know where home was or how I would know it, but the longing was a constant, insistent pain. At times the wolf threw back its head and howled mournfully, giving voice to my despair.

I began to notice a black shadow out of the corner of my left eye, a shadow that vanished when I turned to look at it fully. It appeared again and again. I found myself mentally arranging my affairs and

118

listing which of my possessions I wanted to give away. *This has got to stop*, I told myself. It was like dying without knowing what was killing me. There were days when I wandered the city streets—not knowing where to go or even where I was.

Then one afternoon I stepped in front of an oncoming car. Tires shrieked as the car skidded to a halt only inches away from me. The driver leaned out the window, white as death, and screamed, "You God-damned nut! Get out of the street!" His words shocked me back to myself, and my face burned as I hurried home.

That black shadow had been a warning. A Native American friend told me later that death appears on the left side. The fact I had seen it so many times, she said, meant that I was moving toward it too soon. She thought I must have an animal ally whose vital force was protecting me. That settled it. The next day I called another friend and got the name of a good therapist, Pat B.

Luckily, Pat had an opening. This time, I started off by telling her about my split between the human and animal worlds. She might as well know up front what kind of crazy she was dealing with.

Pat settled into her armchair and listened intently. She was from the Kentucky mountains, and her strong southern accent reminded me of my Aunt Willie. Her open and warm face harbored a pair of shrewd brown eyes that took in everything. The first question she asked seemed like an echo of my first therapist.

"What was your relationship with your daddy like?"

I sat with my legs out straight and my hands stuffed into my pockets and talked briefly about the incest as if I were speaking of someone else. It's best to be frank, I thought.

"I can see from your body that you're armored all down the front of you—do you know what I mean?"

"That's where I put my fear?"

"It's not just fear, hon. It's terror. People don't get to be that armored just by being afraid. You've had adrenalin pumping into you for most of your life. That paranoia is not only keeping people out, it's what protects you right now. I'm not about to mess with that until we find out more about what's going on with you. How much have you explored the incest experiences?"

"Not at all."

"How long ago did it happen?"

"About twenty-five years ago, I guess."

"Jesus," she said quietly. "What do you think that wolf of yours is going to do when we start digging into this?"

"It's protected me all these years, I guess it will protect me now."

"Well, I think when we start dealing with this issue, you may find that your feelings about being part animal and part human may start to change."

"God, that would be wonderful!"

"How much do you remember about what happened? Any details pop into mind or is it pretty vague?"

"Some details," I said. "But not much."

"We'll take it slow. Don't push on it. Just remember this is pretty explosive stuff, so let's take it easy. Okay?"

Okay, I thought. I left the office feeling more hope than I had in years.

That night I dreamed I was in a house with friends, people I knew in the dream but didn't recognize as anyone I'd met in real life. We were walking from one room to another. A dog that looked like a wolf was there with its puppy. I must have moved too quickly as I passed because the dog grabbed my left hand in its teeth, hard enough to hurt. I had to talk quietly and gently to it, reassuring the animal I would not hurt it or its puppy. I talked until the dog released my hand and sat back.

I woke up in the darkened room, feeling a pain in my hand like teeth marks. I mulled the dream over, then fell back asleep. And dreamed the same dream again. This time, the dog looked like a silver-gray wolf. Once again it grabbed my hand, and I had to talk to it until it released me. I carried the puppy outside the house, knowing the wolf-dog would follow. I woke up, rubbing my hand.

When I told Pat about the dream, she was silent for a moment, then asked, "Who do you think the wolf is?"

I didn't know what to say. I'd never thought of the wolf as being anyone, only itself.

"Let me get at this another way," she said. "In the incest family, like the alcoholic family, there's usually one person set up to be the bad guy."

"That was my dad," I said. "We all had a hard time with him."

"So we've got your daddy over here," she gestured with her left hand, "as the villain. Who's over on the right side as the good one?"

"That would be my mom. We all tried to protect her."

"Right. And here are you kids—and especially you as the oldest daughter—right in the middle. Now your daddy is putting out all this primitive sexual energy at you. What's your momma doing?"

"Working away from home. And fighting with my dad over us."

"So it's your daddy's energy that rules the house."

"I'll say. Even though Mom would tell us to stand up to him, she'd always back down."

"And you were the one that was home the most," Pat said.

"Yes, me and my sister. By that time, my brother was in high school and stayed away from the house as much as he could."

"And your momma is away, too. Your daddy's not getting enough focus. It's like a little kid with a lot of primal needs being left out in the cold. So he turns to you. Now that puts you in a real bind, doesn't it?"

I nodded. "I can't let my mother know what's going on, and I can't understand why my father is doing all this."

"But you don't dare say no to him."

"No. I was afraid he'd push me out or break up the family. He used to ignore me sometimes because I wouldn't show him enough affection. I never really liked him, but I had to give him some attention, so he wouldn't turn to my sister. I had to protect her."

"So you called in your magic wolf as your ally to help you guard the secret. A primitive animal to protect you from your daddy's primitive energy. Don't you see whose power the wolf is guarding from the family?"

I looked at her in silence.

"Yours," she said.

I didn't answer. The idea seemed impossible; I had no power. I had never stood up to my father, so I must be weak.

"You weren't protecting your mother just from your father's power, you were also protecting her from yours. Your sexual energy, your ability to see what was going on. That's what you're armored against—the power of your own truth."

"But those dreams—is the wolf telling me to stop?"

Pat studied my face for a moment then asked, "Are you going to?"

"It's too late," I said. The words brought a rush of fear.

"How are you going to let the wolf know?"

121

"I'll say it's all right for us to do this. It will listen," I said firmly.

"All right. In the next couple of weeks, let's work on understanding your family system a little better. Also, I'd like you to think about joining an incest survivors' support group. There are some good ones run at the local hospital here. If I give you a number, do you feel comfortable about calling and looking into it?"

"All right," I said, although I wasn't sure about it.

I had trouble sleeping the next few nights, but there were no more dreams. We worked slowly on understanding how the relationship between my parents supported the incest. I remembered that during the time the incest was going on, my mother had fallen in love with the doctor she worked for. I had been glad for her then, I told Pat. Since things had been so rough with my dad, I thought maybe she would be happy.

"I'll say," Pat commented grimly. "Your dad's pressure was off her and onto you."

"No, you don't understand." I felt a jolt of anger. "She didn't have much with my dad."

Pat didn't argue, but I could tell from her face that she wanted to say more.

It took me three weeks to work up the courage to call the hospital. They said an incest survivors' group was starting the next week, but I could come to an introductory session the following night. All right, I thought, that doesn't sound so bad.

There were eight of us who showed up in the hospital outpatient center. The group was led by a facilitator who told us that just because one of us shared an incest experience with the group, none of the rest of us had to say anything if we didn't want to. I felt they were treating us a little like children.

The first person to speak was a friend of the group leader. She hesitated for what seemed like a long time and then said, "I've never told anyone about this, but when I was nine years old, my cousin abused me sexually. It only happened once, but I've always felt there was something wrong with me ever since." She went on to describe how she had finally come to admit what had happened and to seek help for herself.

I was next. Emboldened by her words, I talked about how much self-contempt I'd always felt and how for the first time I was connecting these feelings to the incest. I was surprised at how easy it was to share with the group. Maybe I had made too much of the whole experience; maybe within a few months I could put it behind me.

The facilitator thanked us both for sharing. At the end of the group meeting, she passed around a sign-up sheet for those interested in attending the next survivors' group. I put my name down. I felt a sudden kinship with the people there, as if we had survived a secret war.

That night I dreamed I was with friends, walking across a field toward a house in the distance. Ahead of us on one side of the path was a red wolf. It was snarling in rage, its fangs bared and its eyes like yellow slits. I turned to one of my friends and exclaimed, "Is that wolf mad!" I started to pass by when the wolf suddenly attacked me. Before I could throw up my arm, it sank its fangs into the side of my neck. We fell heavily to the ground, and I screamed for help.

Then, in the abrupt shift of dreams, it was suddenly twenty-five years later. I was trying to remember if the attack had really happened or if I had only imagined it. In the dream, my friends suggested looking through back issues of the local paper; an incident like that would surely have been reported. I went to the library and after a little digging found the story. Only in the newspaper version, I had been a child of ten or eleven at the time of the attack, while in my own recollection I had been an adult. That's odd, I thought. The story went on. Because the wolf was thought to be rabid, I was started on a series of rabies shots. But before the series could be completed, *I had died!* Stunned, I put the paper down. How could that be? I was still alive....

When I told Pat about the dream, she shuddered and pushed her chair back.

"God, hon, that's a chilling story. It's like you've got your daddy fastened onto your neck. That terror you feel underneath, the power you have to blow your family apart—do you see why you split yourself into animal and human?"

"I'm not sure."

"Babe, as a human being you could tell the secret—but as an animal, *you couldn't talk.*"

I felt as though someone had seized my stomach and wrenched it. I pressed my arms tightly against my middle and bent over, trying to breathe. Pat put her arm around me and made me lie down.

"Just keep breathing," she said. "Keep breathing deep. That's it. We really hit something that time, didn't we? Just keep breathing—through your mouth. Your body just threw all its defenses in there. Put your hands over your stomach and press in. Does that feel a little better?"

"Yes."

She waited until I could sit up again, then said, "You gave the wolf all your power, all your aggression to keep the family safe. It helped you stay sane and alive all these years because it's all right with you for an animal to have that primitive energy. You told the wolf not to let anyone close to the secret; you didn't know then that meant you, too."

"But I have to get in, Pat." I was cold and frightened. "I have to."

"Hon, I think you already have. That little girl didn't die; you used an old magic to change her into a wolf. And now you're starting to call her back again. Little kids under the kind of pressure you lived with often need some kind of magic to survive. It's one of the ways they can feel powerful even if it's only in their own heads. Now it seems like you're getting strong enough to handle the truth without magic."

"But I'm no good without that wolf. I'm no good." I leaned against her. The pressure in my chest made it hard to breathe. I took in gulps of air and suddenly blurted out, "My mother couldn't have known, she *couldn't* have! It means she let it happen—how could she let it happen?"

Pat simply held me. I hadn't cried for myself in years, and now I felt like a little girl sobbing. For the first time, the wolf wasn't there.

\* \* \* \*

In the old days, the Cree Indians prayed for their children to receive the courage, stamina, and wisdom of the wolf. It is a good prayer. I will need all three as I begin to face the memories buried so deeply all these years. I have a long way to go yet. I have stopped visiting or talking with my parents until I work through some of my feelings. Now when I greet my wolf, we salute each other from our separate kingdoms. But I will take the gift of that wolf's spirit with me for the rest of my life.

124

**Laura Baugh:** I am a free-lance writer, editor and poet. For years I have struggled with being blocked in my writing and in my life, not knowing that what had happened to me was incest. Then I realized that to go deeper in my writing, I would have to open up the deeper part of myself I had sealed off. The odyssey has been more harrowing and more liberating than I could ever have imagined. I have confronted both parents about the incest and taken a long step toward healing.

# A Requiem for Mary

It happened on the southeast corner of Main Street a few weeks before Christmas. Part way down the block a Salvation Army worker in a black uniform was ringing a cowbell. Shoppers stopped and put some extra change in the kettle. Cold biting wind always swooped down on anyone at that corner. Wind from the North Pole was made colder by the nearby river. Snow flakes swirled and melted on the sidewalk, obscuring the vision of pedestrians and motorists. Heavy traffic roared across the iron-laced bridge down Main Street.

The corner of Main and Broadway was a blind corner. The Public Service Building went flush to the sidewalk. In the tiny waiting room, bus commuters waited out of the cold wind, peering anxiously through windows fogged with moisture. They could see the bus only as it came to the intersection, and then would dash out across the street, so as not to miss it.

A heavy truck raced across the bridge, turned right and hit Mary. She fell—like a rag doll. The driver heard or felt a thump and backed up to see what happened. The wheels ran over Mary, crushing the life out of her.

Wakes for children were held in their parents' homes then. I went to her home on Oak Street with my mother. Mary's mother met us at the door. Her hair had turned snow-white overnight. She saw me, gave a cry, knelt down and smothered me with an embrace.

I feel guilty that I'm alive and Mary is dead. Mother wants me to submit to the charade that I am Mary to this strange woman, and I'm not.

Mary is in a coffin near the south bay windows in the living room. She is dressed in her white First Communion dress, with a white lace veil on her head. Her hair is curled and a white rosary is entwined in her waxy fingers.

This is a stranger, I think. Is it Mary? I look carefully to see where the truck ran over her, but there are no marks at all. I guess it hit her in the back.

The living room is full of crying women. I'm the only little girl

126

here and want to run away. I don't know where my mother is.

A woman takes me to the kitchen in the back of the house where Mary and I used to go for a snack. Several women are sitting at the table, talking and drinking coffee. They discuss me. "She used to play with Mary." I think "used to"?

Then the strange woman says, "You'll want to see Mary again." I don't. I don't *ever* want to see Mary. *That* isn't Mary. I wonder if I will be like that wax doll someday, like Mary. Reluctantly, I am led back to the coffin. The mourners part as we pass through, and they look at me as if to say, why is she living and Mary dead.

I look closely at the wax doll in the box. Has she moved since I saw her last? I look at her eyes and lips—still closed. I come to the conclusion she'll never move again. And she can't because she is a big wax doll.

As Mother and I finally leave, Mother tells Mary's mother that I'll come to see her. In fact, she told Mary's mother that until I was in college. I never returned. I wanted to run from what I didn't understand. How could I comfort Mary's mother? I wasn't Mary. It wasn't my fault that I was alive and Mary was not.

Behind Mary's house in the backyard was a white picket fence. On it, still drying, were the plums and grapes that we had placed there last summer to see how long it would take for them to become prunes and raisins. They died too, I guess. We never found out.

I had to go to the funeral at the Cathedral. A huge vaulted ceiling was covered with gold gilt and dark pictures. Pillars like round trees obstructed our view. We sat on the aisle halfway back. Everybody cried but me.

Throughout the Latin service I looked at the huge scene of God on the wall behind the altar—sitting in judgement, with a white beard and a stern face, like a grandfather. Angels floated about on white clouds in the blue sky of Heaven. Below were anguished faces of devils with pitchforks stabbing the sinners in the Hell fire. Jesus was on the cross somewhere in between. How it all fit together, I didn't know. There was no solace in the scene for me.

I was not allowed to forget Mary's death. I had to wear her clothes for years... I remember her Easter bonnet, a blue straw poke bonnet with blue grosgrain ribbon. I did not like it. I thought I wouldn't have minded having Mary's bike as I had wanted one so badly.

In those days I thought the resurrection would happen immediately. When Elmer, our little rabbit, died, we put him in a cigar box and had a burial, singing the old Latin Requiem. We dug a hole by the tomato plants and buried him. I stayed after the others left and watched for him to come out of the box. After the third day, I finally came to the conclusion that Elmer would not come back from the dead.

So I knew Mary, my little playmate, wouldn't either.

Forty years later.

I look back at this incident. Why was it that Mary's mother should lose the daughter she loved so dearly and that my mother had not nurtured me with her love? What would have happened if I were the one run over by that truck? Then I realized that in reality all these years I've been the wax doll in the coffin wearing a First Communion dress and clutching the rosary. I wondered that if Elmer and Mary never came back from the dead, would I? I have been wearing a dead girl's clothes all my life. Mary lives even now in the heart and memory of her mother, while I am dead to mine.

This requiem is not for Mary. It is for me.

\* \* \* \*

This story is true. It happened when I was seven, when I think the incest began. But I had been rejected long before by my mother and family. Mary was my first friend. When I was about 12, I told a priest in confession and he said to tell my mother and it stopped. We were a very religious family. No one ever said a word about it again. At the age of 16 or 17 I vowed never to marry in order to expiate my terrible sin. At the age of 23 I entered the convent to continue this expiation. For 25 years I continually broke down but could not leave as I thought I would go to Hell if I did.

At the age of 49 I fell in love for the first time in my life and my memories came flooding back. With the help of my therapist I broke out of my prison and now am living by myself. I found an incest survivor group and VOICES (the Chicago-based organization Victims Of Incest Can Emerge Survivors).

I have great anger towards God and the Church. I am in the process of tearing out from myself the God, who is Judge and Prosecutor, a God I have feared all my life.

It is still hard. Even recently I told a priest about the incest in order to get his approval, and instead he felt sorry for my perpetrator.

My perpetrator died years ago and I don't know if he is in Hell or Purgatory. I have prayed for him for years. When I finally talked to my family, one pretended I said nothing, another thought I was crazy, and another told me she has problems, too, and mine were not bad at all. Incest happens in a dysfunctional family, and even now all my family members and their children are affected adversely. I have tried to help them understand and improve their own relationships, but cannot. I can only help myself. This saviour complex in me dies hard. Taking care of myself comes first. It makes me sad that my family can never be a family for me, in the sense of loving and nurturing. But I am lucky to have my loving friends. They have given me my only sense of worth. Without them I could not have left the convent and begun a scary new life in mid-life.

To look at the future it is necessary to live with hope. I hope to do all those things I have always wanted to do, such as to write, to travel, to own a home and a little puppy.


**Annie**: I have moved back home after many years' absence to become reconciled with my aging parents before they die. My mother is trying to make up to me for the hurt. The perpetrator was my grandpa, who died long ago. I am trying to help battered women in my area.

# Journal Entry

5/13/80

It's been over a month now. One week of emotional hysteria. One week of parents' loving support. Two weeks of happy go lucky jazz festival with only minor frights. Suddenly it's day to day life. The paranoia is heightening. It's much more realistic than emotional. Hiding places everywhere. Total vulnerability. No control of one's own destiny. At any moment a madman could do whatever he pleased to me (not even a madman, a supposed "normal" man, with a job, a family). Afraid to take a shower. As soon as the sun sets, it's time to turn on the TV—illiterate company, background noise. Afraid to walk about the house—someone might be waiting in another room for me. Still very afraid to be alone. The streets are like an open minefield. Must watch your step every way you turn. News release last week—reported rapes are up 50% from last year. Where has respect and morality gone? Respect for others and their lives? My sense of hearing is very acute—ice crackling in a glass, rustling papers—normal sounds that usually go unnoticed now are of prime importance. A continual state of fight or flight must be unhealthy for the body. Waiting for something to happen—where, when, how. It's as if it's just around the corner. Had to start leaving the lights on at night again. I can understand the initial emotional hysteria—but I don't understand these delayed reactions. It's no longer reactions to the actual crime, but it's a fear of future crimes. A friend called upon me to give initial support to one who had just been raped. I could understand the unprovoked crying outbursts, the anger—the rage that people have the balls, no, so little respect for others to do such a thing. The only comfort I could give was to say I understand and it does get better. But I don't understand this step, or what will come next.

**Beverly J. McClendon:** After my rape I spent four years on my personal recovery, on self-growth and on helping others through local and national anti-rape work. Currently I am living in the Alaskan wilderness in a safe, healthy, nurturing environment in which I don't have to continually fear the threat of a guerrilla attack from men.

# Now, What?

A halting dawn
breaks over a barren battlefield;
the warriors all,
ghosts and bones.
Weeds sprout amid the debris.
The war is long over
and I am still alive.

I expected a hero's death
with courage, valor,
and posthumous rigamarole.
I expected to be an unknown soldier
loyal to inevitability
true to the cause
regretful that I had but one life to give
in the name of honor, glory,
world with an end,
amen.

I have studied well
the art of dying nobly.
I made no preparations
to live post-war.


**Bridey Collins:** I am a poet, essayist and writer of fiction. Recently, I have finished my first novel, "The Working Babies," and am seeking a publisher. It relates the story of a young woman's struggle with and ultimate survival of child abuse.

# Eleven P.M.

In a town
where one minute's walk
takes me to fields that yawn wide
to the woods,
things that happen to others
seem closer.
Silence settles here
like a net.

Ever since the woman was raped,
I go no farther than the river,
stand on the bridge
to watch the moon's hazy bowl
tip black soup
into the air.

I want to throw the bones of the rapist
from this bridge,
see his blood move with the river
under the ice.
I have been accused of anger:  Yes,
and like the tongue of a shapeless bell,
I have no place to strike.

Going home,
the dog and I move carefully
through frozen air.
Brittle as ice, we are
looking for danger.
We could be so easily broken
by the wind's cold knife,
by the the knife of a stranger's eyes.

**Guri Andermann:** I was raped nearly twelve years ago, and it is still affecting my life. I had never heard of a rape crisis center, neither my friends nor I wanted to discuss it, and my therapist told me it was no big deal. As a result of the amazing silence around the rape, it festered inside of me for a long, long time. When I started to read feminist books on male violence and began to work to end violence against women (only two years ago), I finally was able to break the silence and throw off its chains.

I stopped writing about the time I started to grapple with the issue of violence, so I have yet to deal with it in my poetry to any major extent.

# The Robbery

They broke in and beat me
over my (sleeping, vulnerable, innocent) head.
I woke, hoping it was a dream.
Faced with reality,
beaten, trapped,
I vowed to struggle.

While I slept,
it held me down.
I couldn't move,
but I screamed my protest
that reality could be so cruel.

They called it a robbery,
although nothing was stolen
except:
my independence
my strength
eyes which looked ahead
the distance of death
peaceful sleep
the car without a ghost in the back seat
streets without shadows
friendliness
rooms with soothing quiet
rooms with comfortable, accepted sounds
tragic headlines of faraway people
men who might be nice
my independence
my strength.

They left and the screaming stopped
but inside I still hear
and wonder:

Will I ever be rich enough
to recover what was stolen?

Still,
beaten by reality,
I vow to struggle;
I scream my protest.

**Karen Brown:** I am a children's librarian, perpetual student in women's history, feminist, activist. When I was assaulted, I looked everywhere for a book that would help me heal, so I'm happy now to be part of such a book. I relied on the support of family and friends, the inspiration of Peggy Placier, and the counsel of my local Rape Crisis Center (which helped even though I wasn't raped). I believe, however, in the power of writing and reading to reach inside, to touch us more deeply than even the closest friend can. Three years later I'm in many ways recovered, but I know for certain I'll always be recovering and I'll always be protesting.

# Raped

*Into each life a little rain must fall.*

You made it pour.
Noah's Ark wouldn't have survived the storm you made!
All in one dark, malicious night,
My tears were rain,
During and after.
Your sperm was hail,
Pelting at my inner thighs and crotch—
Everywhere it touched.
(I bathe 7 times a day now,
And douche 3 times daily,
But still can't rid myself of your stench.)

You took my humanity
Away from me
That night,
Along with the choice to bear children.
(Yes, you bastard,
The doctors say you really
Ripped me apart,
Physically,
As well as mentally.)

You took away my trust in men—
ALL men.
I look at every man out of the corner
Of my disfigured eye
(Yes, the damage you did
With your knife
Was permanent—)
And wonder . . .
Did you hurt a woman today

Last night
Last week
Last year?
Will you later today
Tomorrow
Next week
Next year?

You took the only thing I truly possessed—
Me,
My self-respect.
I have broken all the mirrors
In my now barricaded apartment.
I talk to no one but
My soul-sisters,
And even in the most casual conversations,
I can't help but wonder . . .
Did a man hurt you?
Do you dream of it
When you are able to grasp sleep?
Do you want to castrate him
With your bare hands,

As I do?
Was it someone you trusted?

Was it your brother?

**Gina Diane Joice:** This poem is an accumulation of experiences.
They are my experiences as well as my mother's and my friends'.
i was assaulted three times before i was sixteen, my mother was
assaulted twice and raped once, and five friends (that i know of)
have been raped.

Unfortunately, this is not all that uncommon. i hope that by
writing this, in some way it helps to inform and enlighten us. i don't
want it to comfort us, though. i don't want anyone to feel comfortable in a society where anyone feels compelled to write work like
this.

# Don't Call Me Chick

My body has always been my traitor,
from the first moment I saw it
open and bleeding—
cut from below like a gutted chicken,
still squawking from a half-wrung neck.

Plucked and naked,
covered with white stubble,
crutch-folded wings,
fat-waddle,
huge hips,
good only for making soup
when you're sick.

Skin all bumpy, yellow,
great staring eyes,
hoarse, high voice,
flaring nostrils,
open beak.

Don't call me chick
you strutting cock.


**Nancy C. Douglas:** Now I am what I always had the capacity to be: ambitious, assertive and feminist, respected by my peers as an intellectual. Going through my late teens in the midwest, I had no peers and had to hide to a degree in appropriate female behavior. My whole life at twenty was being victimized in various ways. The only sexual victimization, however—which went off and on for five years—was by a friend/lover/teacher who appreciated my mind and talent at the price of sex on demand and physical abuse that eventually rendered me sterile. I used to write a lot of poetry—now I try to change society with my prose.

# Untitled

I

We all know you wear a dick.
Shall I incite you
flush you into the open?
Shall I threaten you,
assert my strength in spite of your violence?
Shall I
Shall I taunt you?
Impotent
hairless eunuch
buttercup balls
puny penis
ugly sore-covered face
stupid
worthy of cattle spit.

Shall I get vengeance?
There is a rabid fox waiting to bite your scrotum.
There is a city night dweller lurking and intending
to slash your penis with a rusty razor.

Shall I humiliate you?
Tie you to a pillory pants down and
bare assed before a laughing crowd
throwing rotten fruit.
Delights of returned agony.

Now we are getting close to the return
to purging the violence in my belly

spin deeper
down further

II

Come on you fucker.
Show your face
I want to torture you
I dare you to come out of the shadows
I won't kill you
watching you live with pain is much more fun.
Come on out
or can you only kill little girls
half your size,
unarmed;
pretty weak victory.

Let's see your illness and anger
meet someone head on
someone with equal anger
equal need to wreak havoc and avenge.

We will set up an arena
a fair fight
impartial judges
no weapons.
Are you ready?
Can you still do it?
Are you even here?
You will get a fair shot at me,
I promise.
But I also warn you
now,
you will lose.

Soon,
push down
further
physical imprints
and untameable wrath
don't get in my way.

Soon, it will be
just one time,
one time too many.
I will lose all sanity
become the wild animal that
would hunt and rend you into pieces
before you can remember who you really are . . .

There is no freedom here
I am still frightened inside my memories.
I know no vengeance
rage alone cannot purge or prevent you.
I know this place,
there is no hope here
there is no life here.


### III


I will not be
caught forever within the violence you have shown me.
I will not
hate you.
I have already hated enough
there is silence between us.
There are tears.
Tears like rivers
like vomit
like lava
like the sea bath that burns the wound and cleans it.

There is a silence
between the wind's chase through the forest leaves.
And in that echo, I remember.

You are the victim and the humiliated
but you are not exonerated.
You may have been hurt,
that is not cause enough to hurt.
You may be deeply damaged by others

I am sorry for your pain.
You,
another frail human being,
I can give compassion
but you are not exonerated.
You
unconscious of your evil
are lethal and dangerous,
and I will disarm you
before giving you my hand.
Our lives are not your privilege
any longer.

This is what I say to you
what is necessary to our survival:
If you come after me
with all your dis-ease and rage,
you cannot destroy  me.
We will dance around
a ritual of power,
an evocation.
In your call once more to dismember life
I will have memory and feeling enough for both of us;
unbinding your violence inch by inch
holding all who may have been lost before.

To stay alive,
you may penetrate me.
But your eyes shall meet mine full and open.
You may take out another weapon then
and choose my death.
I am not ready to die
and will be scared.
Sad, that these are unfair odds,
it could have been person to person
heart to heart.

If you choose to kill me
make no mistake
I will fight for my life.

If your violence prevails
I will look you full in the face again
knowing it is you who are doomed.

**M. Fox:** Being survivors of incest asks that we live with the courage of heroes—but without the fanfare. And it asks that we do not die but instead be full with the dance.

# Stories My Body Tells

I didn't remember anything about the incest until March of last year, when, in the middle of the night, I began to get back pieces of memories of physical feelings that terrified me. For over a month I slept only 1 to 1 1/2 hours a night because of this. At that time I was able just barely to hold onto the fragments of these feelings, not to put them together or to make sense out of them.

Now I need to say what happens to me when I talk about the incest. It makes me feel sick to my stomach, and if I go on enough, I get stomach cramps, sometimes so I can hardly walk, and then diarrhea, which can last several days. I often shake and feel very cold, or else various parts of my body feel hot, and they can vibrate. So can the room. Sometimes my ears ring. Once I got so tense at talking so much, I felt unable to move at all. It took me 2 hours to get up and leave, and I only did it by telling each muscle separately to move.

I often feel it's my talking and thinking about the incest that makes it real, that it's not real if I don't do these things. In other words, forgetting about it meant it never really happened. In fact a lot of my first year of remembering has been a struggle over the reality of these very painful memories.

Another thing that can happen when others are talking about incest is my getting upset—hurt or angry—because "that's my father you're talking about." No matter what he did, I still care about him. I even still love him, though I often wish I didn't because that would be easier.

Next I want to talk about other people's reactions to my talking, even very generally, about what happened to me, the incest, and the process of remembering it. Usually I feel horror, disgust, and a whole lot of fear coming to me from them, and it does seem to be directed toward me, rather than toward the incest itself. I feel people going far away from me in their feelings, if not physically. In fact many people I thought were my friends no longer want anything to do with me since I've become involved in this process of recovering my past.

145

Yes, I know very well it's because of how scary and time consuming it is. And, yes, this process is likely to change our lives quite drastically. It's certainly done these things to me. Then, too, I know we all have buried some of our most painful past experiences, and for many women these are likely to be sexual experiences as children or teen-agers, most of them with males close to or even within our own families.

Finally to get down to what actually happened to me: I had sexual experiences with my father from at least age 3 until I was almost 11. Since I'm now 40 years old, I forgot about these for some 29 years. The first thing I remember is Daddy masturbating my younger sister and me with a washcloth while giving us a bath. This was a completely pleasant experience for me, and it happened regularly. I also remember a tickling game where he eventually put his finger in my vagina, which I didn't like. When I asked him to stop, he'd always say "in a minute." His keeping on a while served to increase my tolerance for this experience. I certainly liked his touching. In fact I liked it a lot, and it seemed there were other things I simply had to accept as inevitably going along with the wanted touching.

I don't remember ever being close to Mother. She always seemed angry with me no matter how hard I tried to please her, and she spanked me often. I didn't feel comfortable being hugged or even touched by her because she felt so stiff and hard, really unyielding. Daddy, on the other hand, held and touched me "just right," our bodies softening and melting into each other. He even masturbated me "just right." If only he'd stopped at that, when I asked him to. He was really tuned in to me emotionally and physically, and that felt wonderful. I know the incest began with his genuinely loving sensitivity and warmth toward me.

From the beginning I sensed Mother was both defeated and quite powerless, while Daddy was spontaneous and feeling, as well as powerful. He was less beaten down by the world and therefore clearly much more alive. And he used his superior power against Mother. In fact I always felt I had more power than she did, perhaps, because in many ways Daddy seemed to prefer me to her. I can see how extremely frustrating it was for Mother to be continually confronted by a small girl who felt this way, especially when it was her job and duty as a mother to love, nourish, and teach me. How could she teach me when I didn't respect her?

When I was about 5 something happened that really frightened me. This is the first memory I managed to recover, and it's still the most terrifying. I'm lying on my back on the living room floor, and Daddy's tickling me, but he's lying on my hips and rubbing himself against my thigh. His weight starts to hurt, and I ask him to get off. He says "in a little while" and goes on a bit. He turns away, then comes back with his pants unzipped and his penis out. The erect penis jutting out of his fly looks gigantic and monstrous to me. In fact this is a picture of my own well-loved father turning into a nightmarish monster before my eyes.

Then he puts his penis in my mouth, and I have trouble breathing and start to choke. I feel I'm being killed, so I close my mouth, of course biting him. He grabs my throat and chokes me to make me open my mouth and let go of him. I see red, then black, and finally vomit, releasing him. He's angry and runs out of the room. I lie there completely gone, floating up near the ceiling looking down at that small child's body lying still, covered with vomit. This is the start of one way I dealt with what happened to me, namely by leaving my body and going very far away. That way I could see what was happening, but I didn't have to feel it as much because it wasn't happening to me.

After a while Daddy came back and was very nice to me. He picked me up and washed me off, put me in his lap and held me and stroked me, saying, "It's all right. Nothing bad's going to happen," and things like that. I feel this pattern contributed to my forgetting about the incest for so long. I simply couldn't maintain in my consciousness 2 such different images of my father, so I wiped out the bad scary one and kept only the good comforting one since I needed that so much.

The things he said to me seem at least as important as what he did. For instance, he always told me I liked what he did no matter what I said or did to contradict this. Sometimes he'd get me turned on by touching my genitals and then stop and say he was done now. He'd ask if I wanted to stop, and I'd tell the truth, no. Then he'd act real reluctant, like he was only doing it to please me, which made me feel I was "badder" than him because he wanted to stop and I didn't.

Daddy used my enjoyment of a small part of the incest to tell me over and over again how I really wanted all of it. I know I still haven't finished sorting out the tremendous confusion involved in this continual mixing up of my pleasure with his, and especially of what felt good to me and things that felt downright painful. A lot happened at night after I'd already gone to sleep, and afterwards he'd often hold and comfort me, saying I'd had a bad dream.

My father had intercourse with me over a period of years. I don't know how old I was when it began. I just remember waking up, or somehow coming back to consciousness, knowing something that felt important had happened to my body and I didn't know what it was. Then I tried to figure it out. Something had been inside me "down there," but what could it be? It was shaped like a piece of broom handle, but softer and not so long. Mostly I felt indifferent to this at first. I didn't like it, but it also didn't hurt very much either.

Then there seems to be a time when I began to realize there was a moral judgement against what Daddy and I were doing, so I started to feel guilty about it and tried to get him to stop. However, there seemed to be no way for me to make him stop as long as I enjoyed part of it, namely the touching. No matter how much I struggled and fought, said no and turned away, he took it as just some kind of teasing game, and went right on, saying "Oh, come on, you know you really like it." And his words were somewhat effective because I had to admit there was indeed one part I definitely did like, the sexual touching. So I felt betrayed by my own body and began to hate her (my body).

At the same time, I started wondering how much Daddy really loved me. Of course he always said he did, but he absolutely refused to believe me when I told him I didn't like something he was doing to me, or even that it hurt. In fact he often laughed when I said these things. This made me doubt my own feelings and perceptions, since as kids we all need to believe our parents. We know we should do what they say and learn from them. Also, I knew he truly loved me, and I could not make sense out of my Daddy doing something extremely unpleasant or hurting me unless it was for some very good reason. At least I don't recall him ever telling me it was for my own good. No, what he always said was that I was only teasing or joking when I said I didn't want to do something.

At last I came to realize Daddy would go on doing those things to me no matter what I felt, said, or did; it seemed to me he'd continue even on my dead body, since he went on so many times on a body I'd long ago left in order not to feel as much of what was

148

happening to me. This realization of my complete powerlessness, especially at the hands of someone I loved and trusted and who said he loved me, made me want to die. I got into hurting my body in order to learn to feel less, especially pain, and to get on the outside some of the hurt I felt inside.

When I was between 5 and 8 an incident occurred involving Mother, too. I was sleeping in bed with her because Daddy was away traveling on his job, something that happened fairly frequently. He came home unexpectedly in the middle of the night and was very angry. He might have been drinking. He and Mother had an argument about sex, and he ended up raping her. She fought and yelled, especially about me being there, but it didn't make him stop. It might even have turned him on. Naturally, I pretended to be asleep. He knew I wasn't and said "You're next" to me.

When he finished with her, she was hurt and exhausted. He turned to me and began touching my nipples and then my genitals in a very rough way that seemed like torture to me. He grabbed onto me quite hard and pulled, twisted and pinched. It hurt a whole lot, but there were also some strong flashes of pleasure. This time I remained passive throughout, and said and did nothing. I also tried unsuccessfully to feel nothing, too. This is my most confusing memory and the one of which I'm most ashamed. When he was done, Mother carried me into my own bed and held and stroked me. She defended Daddy by saying he didn't mean to hurt me, that he couldn't help himself and that he was really a good man.

I have another memory that's the most painful one. It's obviously only a fragment, beginning with me already being very frightened by something that's happened. I'm curled up with my knees pulled up to protect my stomach and my head down with my hands and arms over it. I'm rocking and moaning. Daddy first crouches over me without leaning, which feels warm and good, even sheltered and protected. Then he begins to force his penis into my anus. It feels like being rammed repeatedly from behind. He holds on to my shoulders, so I can't move away from him. This memory disappears into so much pain I am as yet unwilling to go into it any further.

In the late spring when I was 10 1/2, I had my appendix out. Despite all comforting, shaming and threats, I cried continuously the whole 5 days I was in the hospital. I was terrified I was going to die because a boy in my 5th grade class had died earlier that year after having his appendix out. It really surprised me to realize how much I didn't want to die, since I'd spent a lot of time wishing I would. Somehow it seemed that in order just to live, that is to want to live rather than to want to die, I had to stop my father from doing those things to me. But of course I had no idea how I could do this. Nevertheless I knew I just had to do it.

After I went home I was very scared whenever Daddy came into my room. Of course at first he was quite nice to me and didn't try anything. Then he started with his usual line, "I'll just touch you a little to make you feel good, and I'll stop whenever you tell me to." I didn't believe him, but, also as usual, I didn't feel I had the power to prevent him. He began very softly and gently, asking if this hurt or that hurt. "No." Naturally, after a while he was leaning on me putting his penis in, and it did hurt, quite a lot more than normally. All of a sudden I realized I was once more back in this position I'd said I never wanted to be in again.

I knew I had to do something or it would just keep happening to me forever, it seemed, so I raised my legs up and back, and kicked him hard. He looked so surprised and said in this hurt, indignant tone, "Hey, you're hurting me," which really got to me. I remembered how very many times I'd said those exact words to him and got back "just a minute," and my anger took over. I really fought Daddy without reservation or without bothering to be afraid of hurting him. In fact I truly wanted to hurt him, and I tried to and succeeded, at least in part.

This time I felt I'd made him angry, and it seemed rather more like rape than just sex when after simply dodging most of my fury, he systematically held me down, worked his penis into my vagina, and went at it. I see that whenever I caused him pain, whether by biting his penis in fear when I was 5, or by expressing my anger at 10, he got angry. But after he'd come he still took the trouble to turn me on by touching me. It was so frustrating and infuriating that he was able to force me to experience sexual pleasure when I also felt angry and hopelessly defeated at the same time. It made me hate feeling at all.

After he knew he'd succeeded in making me feel turned on, he told me I should to kiss his penis because that's where my pleasure really came from. I just wanted to get rid of him and be left alone, so I began to comply, though I was disgusted by his penis, let alone putting my lips on it. When I actually felt him with my lips, I couldn't stand it and threw my head back then forward, with my lips drawn back and my teeth open. I clamped them shut underneath, on his soft, hairy, smelly balls. I still feel some satisfaction at hearing his outrageous scream and quickly aborted jerk away, as I'd locked my jaws firmly closed. He hit at my face and head with his fists, but I was oblivious because this wasn't a conscious decision I'd made to act. Instead it came from somewhere deep inside me as a last desperate measure to try to protect myself. He ended up moaning, sobbing, and begging me to let go. Just as I had been gone from my body when we had sex, so I was also absent on this occasion. Neither his orders nor appeals could move me to release him. There was simply no consciousness left in my body to be either ordered or appealed to.

Next I see a shiny black wing-tip oxford swinging from the left into the back of my neck, and a dark sock and part of a navy trouser leg with it. The blow shocked me into unlocking my teeth. I'm not sure I ever saw who kicked me, but I suspect an uncle who lived near us. I lose this memory here, perhaps because I lost consciousness. Again I don't know for sure. But during the course of my remembering, a certain point on the back of my neck has become very sensitive, even to the touch of a pillow. I truly wonder what possible conversation could have ensued between Daddy and my uncle over the most peculiar position my uncle inadvertently witnessed him in with me.

I felt really bad about myself because of how much I'd wanted to hurt Daddy and that I'd actually tried to do it, had in fact done it. In my mind that made me worse than him, because I knew he didn't really think what he was doing hurt me, whereas I knew I was hurting him, and that's exactly what I wanted to do.

My finally fighting back without reservation was a big step in getting my father to stop molesting me, which was essential for my own survival. He came to me only once more, months later, saying I used to really love him and like what he did. He asked to try just one more time to see if I didn't still like it after all. I knew what he said was true and felt if he could still make me like any part of what he did, I remained in his power. It seemed I had to let him try one more time in order to see whether I'd finally succeeded in my struggle not to feel anything. Again he was slow and gentle, asking how this and that felt, but it was completely clear to us both that I was not turned on by anything he did. So I won the struggle, and he didn't bother me again. But of course I also gave up something very important, namely my own natural connection with my body, her feelings, in fact, my own feelings.

Daddy was able to ignore and discount totally whatever negative feelings I expressed, whether by saying no, screaming and crying, or by turning away and even struggling and fighting to protect myself. Yet I still don't see him as violent, but rather as having an incredibly arrogant belief in the rightness of his view that I really liked all of the incest because I liked being masturbated. It wouldn't work to lie and say I didn't enjoy anything because I knew he was tuned in enough to me to know when I felt pleasure. Logically, then, he must also have been tuned in enough to realize when I didn't feel pleasure. In fact this is proven by him stopping the incest when I finally succeeded in not feeling any pleasure. He neither tried to convince me I did, nor did he approach me sexually again. His being unable to make me feel pleasure clearly ended the game for him, just as I'd felt sure it would.

How could he totally discount my pain and yet be so sensitive to my feelings of pleasure? It must be because my pleasure was very much in his self interest in continuing the incest. Nevertheless I don't recall him repeating the acts that gave me absolutely no pleasure, namely oral and anal intercourse. I also think the most painful part of what he usually did was emotional rather than physical.

It is surely a subtle and refined kind of torture to have your own body's pleasant sensations made a justification for someone to do repeatedly to you many different acts that range from unpleasant to downright screamingly painful. To come to orgasm crying out "NO NO NO NO" with each shudder of your body appears to me an ultimate kind of betrayal.

A very important result of the intensity, both good and bad, of this incestuous relationship with my father is my seeing myself as crazy. Perhaps this is more accurately described as a blurring of boundaries. When I feel things strongly, especially bad feelings, and then see or hear others expressing something similar, I feel they've taken on my feelings and are expressing them for me. When I'm vibrating, I tend to experience the vibrations as coming from the room and floor.

When I'm feeling things this intensely, it's hard for physical sensations to get through into my awareness. Usually I become conscious of discomfort or pain completely nonspecifically. Then I have to go through a checklist of possibilities to determine, first of all, if its cause is inside me rather than outside, such as noise. At least when I ask my body if this is what she needs, I do get definite answers. I ask about cold, heat, hunger, thirst, need to pee, getting sick, need to change positions.

I've also developed a routine for panicked freak out, which goes like this. I say "ORIENT" to myself very loudly, and then open my eyes to take in where I am, touching the surrounding furniture, rug, ground, etc., remembering what place this is. It is often helpful to find out what time it is and, therefore, about how long I've been "out of it." Sometimes I review the sequence of events, thoughts, and feelings that got me freaked out and invariably find it very logical. This is dangerous, since it tends to lead me right back into the same freak out. Then I order myself to "STOP" and usually get up and do something, which inevitably helps.

I don't judge all, or even most of these experiences as bad, but I certainly do have to be careful about when and where I allow myself to go into them, and with whom. And of course I can't always control this. Sometimes I'm only aware of it when I'm already well into it.

The main long-lasting negative effect I recognize from the incest is my deep feeling that I myself am bad in some very basic sense. I feel this regardless of how much I try or how hard I work to do useful and worthwhile things. There are times when what I really want is for someone to say to me over and over again, for days and weeks, maybe even longer, "you are good." And, yes, I am working at doing that for myself with affirmations.

Another important effect is my continually doubting my own feelings and intuitions, having always to justify and prove them even to myself. I also have a very real fear of being vulnerable, especially with another person, and this relates directly to close relationships and love.

I am working at healing myself by trying to be as conscious as I can of how my body feels, since I've spaced this out quite completely for some 35 years. When I'm aware of a physical sensation, I try to respect it and to act on it. I change positions more often when lying or sitting, for example, instead of working on increasing my endurance of discomfort. I'm trying to be more gentle with my physical self.

153

I've been working on being my own mother, which is certainly what I feel I want, comforting myself, even stroking myself and telling myself I'm good and the like, just as I've done for my daughter for the 10 years I've had her. I can really get into feeling both sides of this, the giving and the receiving, and it does seem to help, once I get past thinking how foolish it appears.

I've realized I don't want to be around men and am making efforts to change my life in this way. Especially I don't want to be touched by men. At this time I'm not going to judge that feeling as good or bad, but right now I want to honor it. So I've left the man I've lived with for 11 years, and we are sharing the care of our daughter year by year.

Quiet is extremely important to me, as is having some long periods of time with no interruptions, so I moved into a little 15-foot hexagonal house up a mountain with no telephone, TV, radio, or stereo. Being outdoors is very positive for me, and a small house keeps me less separate from the weather and the outside environment. I slept outside in a tent last year until November in the British Columbia Interior and took a 5-day hike alone the last week of October. Despite a lot of rain I loved it and made 44 miles with a heavy pack. For once I felt I belonged on this earth, that she could be (and sometimes is) a good connection for me. The moon and stars are even more important for me than the sun, and I've stayed up or awakened many times to sing and chant to them. My daughter loves to do this with me.

I try to do exercises and run every day, and meditate. I fast one day a week and have stopped eating meat. I have 2 things I wear for protection. One is a copper bracelet I made after seeing it in a meditation. Sometimes I lie naked on the ground facing a certain way into the sun with my arms and legs outstretched. Last year I swam in the river where I lived in British Columbia in mid-March, when there was still snow on the ground. I always spoke to the waterfall I ran past on a dirt logging road every morning. With my arms out I asked her to lend me her grace and power, and I asked for other things I needed.

Yes, I acknowledge the uniqueness and seeming craziness of a lot of this, and I certainly don't expect anyone else to do what I'm doing. But it feels extremely important for me in this second half of my life to honor as many of my newly emerging desires as I can, even when I don't understand them or know exactly either where they come from or where they're leading me.

I know for sure that a minimum personal requirement for me is belonging to an incest survivors' support group, which is why I left B.C. and came to Oregon. I spent 2 1/2 months traveling around Vancouver, Oregon, northern California, and western Montana asking questions about groups and programs around incest, and I learned a great deal. I was very fortunate to be able to join a survivors' group in Eugene, Oregon. There I had the experiences of talking about what happened to me and having it draw the other group members closer to me because they felt what I said helped them. This was in strong contrast to what usually occurred when I said anything where I lived in B.C. and my words always seemed to drive people away from me because of their own disgust and fear.

I have a long-range goal of setting up a healing center in the country where women can come, with our children if necessary. We could live there for varying lengths of time and go crazy in order to heal ourselves, as I feel I have had to do and am still in the process of doing. There would be a community in many different stages of healing ourselves, using all kinds of methods and newly created techniques, many devised by our own community, both alone and together.


**Pegasis Touch:** Incest happens in all segments of society, not just in poor or socially isolated families. My family, for example, is middle class. My mother is of English background and was trained as a teacher. My father is Irish Catholic and worked as an engineer. I was raised in a suburb of an eastern city with a younger sister and brother.

I am now 45 and live in Ashland, Oregon, with my 15-year-old daughter. I am a lesbian interested in writing, spirituality, music, backpacking and sewing. I work taking care of old people in their homes.

# Healing

# My Father Is Dying

I say to my sister, Does he ask about me?
Her eyes are deep fury, a storm at night you can't see through,
a chill wind. She thinks I have caused all this.

I feel him calling me today. I am living in the mountains in a
house without a phone. I have saved the afternoon for walking, my
mind still floating on last night's dream. I was swimming, but not
getting anywhere. Finally a woman about my mother's age said,
You have to dive deeper.
I leave to walk along the river and I can hear him: a weak, feeble
call from a hospital bed, from the empty gloom of his apartment,
stale air thick, waiting for death.

He wants me to see the way he looks now, no longer bathing,
refusing to dress. He wants to look at me with forlorn eyes silently
accusing, This is what you have done to me. His beautiful thick
white hair shaved for radiation treatments. I can't imagine him
bald. White hair even in his thirties, rolling back from his head like
ocean waves. White and full as summer clouds above eyes deeper,
more vacant than sky.
When I look at the pictures of him as a young man, so handsome, muscular, it is hard to imagine, much less accept, what he did
to me when I was three.
Maybe he will be soft and blubbering, asking my forgiveness,
as if I have the power to erase the indelible.
Maybe he'll send for me, instead of coming to my room as he
did when I was fifteen; my mother behind him, waiting at the door,
smiling, nodding encouragement. Yes, this is one of Alcoholic
Anonymous' Twelve Steps: I will make amends to those I have
harmed unless to do so would cause them more harm.
I was lying on my bed, reading. Who knows what more harm
would have been? He was sorry he said. He would never do it
again. He lay on top of me and cried. Sorry, sorry. I knew nothing
of boys, didn't know what I already knew of men, of him. But

something was wrong. My body stiffened; I couldn't breathe. My head raced: I wish he'd stop, why's he crying, I hate him for being so weak. I was embarrassed—my mother was watching from the door. Now I realize that though he drank again and again, he never broke his word to me: he never did it again.

My sister's shrink says someday my incest "experience" will be just another characteristic, like the color of my eyes. Blue-green, combination of his, my mother's hazel. I am just beginning to realize all my eyes have seen.

Yesterday I rode my bike through the village up onto the road that snakes through Osha Canyon. Like being a kid again—dirt roads and fat tires, a sense that you can go anywhere, the world golden as sunlight on the pines. And then around a bend everything crazy, ravaged, a war in the forest. One lone ponderosa, a tall one, still standing above a field of twisted limbs, broken branches, hundreds of twenty and thirty foot trees strewn across the battlefield, left for dead. I try to ride past them, but can't. Both sides of the road heaped with remnants of trees.

I recognize the work of loggers, their smug definition of power: revving up a saw and cutting the biggest tree just to watch it fall. The canyon narrows; the sun is gone. I turn around and pedal fast so there is only a blur of green, all the time wondering how long it will take for this one slope to grow again.

I think he is close to death. This is why I hear him calling as I walk along the river below my house. It is always cold in the canyon this time of year. When the sun shows, I climb up to a warm patch of earth and write. Otherwise I walk.

Downstream, further into the canyon where the steep slopes change to blunt rock, lined granite. The colors! Black, grey, green, copper and sand, spotted with rust and pale green lichen. The sea was once here. All this land underwater. I am diving deep, walking downstream where the canyon opens and another village begins.

Maybe he will speak to me as he always does; TV on, doing a crossword puzzle, How's your truck running; how's the weather up there? Almost always ending in an argument. Why am I cleaning houses; why don't I give up being a writer—only one percent make it; why am I going to Alaska; why am I going on the bike trip alone—I'll be raped on the lonely road. He understands the special fear I should have about rape, but not the anger. Why do you have to write about *that*? Why do you have to be so angry? We haven't spoken in two years. Except last month when I called to tell him I knew. A short conversation: I didn't want to hear the denial I heard slung at my mother all those years—It's all in your head; you're crazy; you don't know what you're talking about.

Hey, he said, excited to hear my voice.

I just want you to know, I began.

Five days later he was in the hospital, blurry vision diagnosed as a stroke, later changed to pressure from a malignant tumor in his brain. My father is dying.

A little three year old lives inside me who understands all this better than I do. Understands a pain so searing she will do anything to avoid it—leave town, quit a job, hurt a lover, a friend. Anything. She understands power and control gained by injuring others. She trusts no one. Not him, not you, not me. We have all failed her. I battle her each day not to be afraid to get up in the morning, to do my work with a sense of purpose, to really feel. Instead of listening to her: Feelings are dangerous. You can only get hurt, or hurt someone you love because you're bad. You can't be trusted. You aren't good enough.

It doesn't matter. Nothing you do matters. There's no point, only circles going round and round. Your only safety is to be alone. You can have the woods, mountains, rivers, sky. The animals will be your friends, but ultimately you will even hurt them. You have before. It doesn't matter. Don't stay anywhere too long. Nothing in this world will feel complete. It's not so bad. You get used to it.

She has not said these words to me consciously. I have not heard them the way I hear this river rushing to its destiny.

But I have lived them.

My three year old went away. We had just begun to talk, to think of each other as friends. She went away the same day my father went to the hospital, before my sister called. I can hear her say, Everyone leaves me, it's ok. The same way I used to say, I'm sure it couldn't be my father.

She is waiting for him to die to reappear. So am I. If I go see him, it may be too much for him. His feelings, his tumor may burst. Does that mean life or death?

I wonder if my sister will speak to me again. Why did you have to tell him? she asks. I don't know why you had to tell him. She is angry because I don't share the daughterly duties: driving him to radiation treatments, cooking, cleaning, dressing him.

I can't bear to face another minute of denial of what has become of my life. How's the weather? Is your truck running all right? I am afraid to look at him and say, This is what you have done to me.

My sister stays with him and his bottle of sleeping pills, so afraid she'll take them, once again try to end her life. She was recovering from an overdose when I told her. I think I have some information that may save your life, I said. She snorted, some little girl in her who knows better.

Nothing can save her life. Not a shrink who smiles when she says she doesn't know what she feels and writes another prescription for psychotropics. Not my mother's prayers. Nothing, but perhaps the chance to rescue my father, the only one of us she hasn't.

Maybe I could save both their lives, help my sister with the chores that are eating her up and my father, my daddy, would talk. Tell me why. Once he said he drank because there's too much pain in the world. I keep thinking, what happened to him? What did some adult force on him? And my three year old answers, Nothing matters. Questions don't change reality. This is what is. She laughs when I say I'm thinking of seeing him—What are you going to say? I came to watch you die, have massive heart failure when you see my face? Or Daddy, Daddy please, oh Daddy. Please please please. Please don't hurt me, please don't die Daddy, oh please?—But maybe I could save their lives. I could be the good girl—No, your sister's already doing that—I could change their lives, I could give them—what you haven't got yourself.

All that has never been said—I begin to understand why communication has always been so important to me. Once and for all get to the bottom of words that just take up air, down to the ones connected to feelings. Her feelings, her words that I have never let out. A way to make it safe for her, that's what all these words

161

pouring out over the years have been. Words dropping like rose petals, a bed of petals to hold her, her words.

I hurt, I hurt so bad, why are you doing this, don't you love me, I must be bad. Now you're smiling at me, I must be ok, but why are you hurting me, why do you give me money, take me for rides alone, why doesn't mommy protect me, why do you want to hurt me, why why why.

I think of how I tried to protect him (why why why)—he was drunk, something must have happened to him; I must have done something to him in a past life. I ask why this happened to me. I don't want to believe it even now.

All the friends who have asked me, Are you sure? You blocked it? You forgot it? My father would *never* have done that to me.

Now I understand my constant fear that lovers will leave me, will find out how bad I really am, why I give them all the power and then hate them for it, why I am so afraid of success and people's demands, why I am never totally myself with other people. I became a "we"—them and whoever I think they want me to be. Please, Daddy.

I still don't want to look at pictures of my father, that handsome young man, and think he did this to me. He took my life at age three and I am waiting for him to die to give it back. Maybe that is why I want to go see him. He will get upset and die and I can be bad forever. I killed my father. I try out these words often. That's what my little one thinks. She came out, I told him, and he's dying.

So die. Let me think this is what happens to men who rape their daughters; men who don't allow their feelings to surface. His brain grows cancerous thoughts; his hair falls out; they are shrinking his brain with radiation. The immaculate man who no longer showers or shaves, pees in his pants, but will not cry. Not until I come see him. He is giving me a power I have wanted all my life—the power to make him feel. A power he mistook, thought he could destroy, takes over. He is trying to give it back to me twenty-eight years later.

I climb to the top of the furthest rock in the canyon. Wind rising up from the valley greets me, this boundary between canyon and village below, pale golden fields, willows blushing purple and red along the river's wide curves, the scrub oaks copper, still holding

162

their leaves, blue mountains in the distance. I see everything now, all the color, soft and subtle, blending into strong landscape, all of myself. My power has nothing to do with him; it is mine. Once again I learn the importance of believing in metaphor.

**Michele Connelly:** My father died shortly after I wrote this story. The biggest part of my healing process came when I realized I could forgive him, and myself for not saying no. My life feels brand new. I am free to be the real me and to love without fear.

# Completing the Ritual

## I

How to say the way shirts burn—
slow to catch, then brightly
flames follow folds of cloth,
leaving stiff lace, none
of the delicacy of wood ash remains.

I remember sitting on a car hood,
my brother flicking matches off a matchbox at me,
and laughing as I hugged my knees
and held my long hair, afraid it would burn
like sparklers all the way to my head.

What did I feel as his shirts became flames—
not glee at him burning,
a rapist in witches' fire,
or what he did to me evaporating as steam.
What burned in my fireplace was me,
the child lost beneath uncharred hair
and skin flickering with fear.

Seven months spent unshriven, forgetting,
the ashes waited in the fireplace.
Today I smelled them chafing my eyelids.
as his shirts had begun eating into my skin:
after five years, even I could not touch myself.

## II

Up a desert wash, two friends,
my husband and I bring frankincense,
a pitcher of water, three candles,
the ashes, the silver charm.
Brambles catch my silk shirt, let go,

leaving no marks.  Unscathed
by this darkness, we approach the circle.

I step inside the rocks and begin.
Here is a candle each, white, red, teal blue:
purity, courage, beauty are lit.
You each stand them in the sand,
protect their faltering flames with your hands.
Incense threads black into the night air.

Silver fish of my birth, this charm
was a gift from my first lover, who
when my mouth burned with whispering
*incest* into *the* first human ear,
his ear, laughed—said
*You must have been a sexy little girl.*
His second gift on my sixteenth birthday—
rape—has masqueraded as these fish
in my jewelry box for eleven years.
This scorched charm is a bond
that won't burn, must be buried.
With it, I scrape the grave site.

Sweeping through the silver bowl of ashes,
my hand rekindles fire there.
Its smoke rises between my fingers,
stings my eyes to tears.
The ashes left feel like clouds look
flying beneath an airplane,
the softness I wanted to touch
as a child in the window seat,
delicate as I dreamed love might be.

I spread the ashes on my arms, my forehead,
make visible what has always covered me.
Bury the rest with the silver fish.
No charm will silence me, rapists.
My childhood is no voodoo doll,
I am pulling out the pins.
Gone is your power over me,

my brother, I bury it here.
Gone, gone, gone, gone.

I cast no spells
in the first ritual of my life.
But think on this, my brother,
the root of sympathetic magic:
to those who do evil, evil returns.

Yes, pour the water, my sister,
help me wash away this cloak of violation.
Hold me, let me tremble in your arms:
the child who could be humiliated, overpowered,
is here entombed.
And her funeral is mine.

You know this death, this letting go,
my sister, and the wingless woman
who rises like a black thread of incense,
enters the body and transforms.
Grief passes
as I free myself, heart and liver,
vagina, vulva, bone, skin and marrow:
I reclaim myself for myself.

I pour water to seal the earth.
I hold and love you each.
Carrying candles, we open the dark
with the tinkling of small bells,
the celebration, the joyous relief,
as we walk back to our lives.


**Pamela Portwood**

# Of Vision Restored: Grandmother Song

*Honeygirl, find warmth wherever you can.*
*Learn to create your own heat.*
—Nellie June Coverdale

I stare into the mirror at eyes
I no longer recognize as my own.
Bleached a desolate gray,
these are my mother's eyes:
squinting through peepholes
opening the doors of my childhood. . .

She finds me napping
hands tucked between my legs,
shakes me awake   voice raging
straps a harness like bandages
around my chest   stomach
forces my tiny arms inside
ties the bundle to the bed.

Every day for two hours I lie:
a cocoon waiting for release,
my eyes hidden behind a levee
of unshed tears.

Grandma comes quietly
she stokes the hearth of my breathing,
her lush mouth sings to me.
Closing the door
she lowers the cracked window shade
slips off her dress,
lies beside me
stroking the curve of my back. . .

My parched eyes fill,
tears spill down my face.
I wrap her love around me like a blanket.


**Amber Coverdale Sumrall:** My grandmother, Nellie June Coverdale, was deeply connected with the spirit in all things. She had a tremendous influence on my ability to love and to heal, and she accepted me unconditionally.

I am a disabled woman of Irish, Dutch and Mohawk ancestry. My work has appeared in *With the Power of Each Breath, A Gathering of Spirit, Sinister Wisdom, The Greenfield Review, Toward Solomon's Mountain, Ikon* and other publications. I believe that silence is one of our biggest obstacles to healing.

# auto-biography

these daze
i'm angry as rusty nails

as angry but not as mean.

i didn't think my anger
could also love
but, i find unwitting allies
 that
    draw down the fire.
i find, too, witting allies—
  magicians.

my anger like heat lightning
  flashes quickly
across pink desert skies
but gives way
  to the waiting night
    and the mouse hop
and the flowering of yucca.

my soul is like a cactus
  moisture glutted
to those who thirst
(gladly i share with those in need.)

my love
  my love
my love drenches
  like desert rain flash floods
out of know-where. here i am!


**Jane Doe #1**

# Pigeons

Through years of deception
we have convinced ourselves
of inferiority,
inadequacy,
dependent on something masculine outside ourselves
for bits of gratitude,
like pigeons
waiting for crumbs,
waiting to be recognized,
waiting to be loved.

Compromise with strangers
seemed like fair exchange
while the truth of our inheritance
lay in fields of fallow
waiting for rain.

But I am not a pigeon.
I thank God I am not a pigeon anymore.

**Peggy Sanders:** I was raped at age 13, but for a long time I perceived the rape as a mature love relationship, kept secret because of societal standards. This misunderstanding became a foundation for distorted attitudes and judgments—the line between right and wrong became a muddy gray. But I was young; circumstances were overwhelming.

Rather than setting me free, the experience secured a bondage that would hinder me for another 13 years. Blatant deception became a justifiable means of gratifying a self-perpetuating hunger for love and reinforcement. Hidden feelings and actions fostered insecurity; emotions demanded refuge. All this while maintaining a veneer of sound resilience.

Unraveling these causes and their effects was the most difficult

170

challenge I had ever faced. But in confronting it, I was strengthened so that I no longer feared the truth or the influence of the past. It was a process of rebuilding character and developing confidence in myself, which together provided me with a security and a faith I had never known before.

# I Did Survive

After eight months of therapy I began to remember the abuse I suffered as a child. I was never able to please my parents, though I tried. According to them, I never did anything right. I have few memories of happy times.

A picture in my mind: I'm three years old. My dad is sliding me up his legs, rubbing me on his crotch. The image fades as nudity suggests itself. "Was that me?" I asked my therapist.

"Yes," she said, "we don't make those things up."

(I am an incest survivor.)

Caught by surprise, my memories horrify me. Anger. I try to pound out my rage on a pillow, but I become my father and the pillow becomes me. I feel helpless and experience my body hurting as the memories emerge in my muscles. One image ends with my mom yelling at my dad: "Stop before you really hurt her!" Those are words I'll never forget. I realize this is only the beginning of my hurt.

My body relives my memories: severe pains in my stomach—remembering he kicked me there. Back pains—beatings. Pain in my vagina, my genitals burning—rape and violation.

I lived from age three to twelve in a brown stucco house. I only recently remembered the ongoing nightmare I lived through there. My mother made me sleep upstairs by myself, while my two brothers slept in the room across the hall. Later, my sisters arrived and had the room downstairs. I was the only one isolated and unprotected—convenient for dad.

* Memory: Dad has me cornered. He is going to beat me. I don't know why. What have I done? I shelter my face with my hands, whimpering. I'm scared he will hurt me again.

* Memory: I'm sick. I don't feel well and I complain to dad. He is suddenly furious, yelling at me. He sticks his penis in my face and tells me now I will have something to complain about . . . The

172

memory abruptly ends there leaving me with terror, nausea, not knowing where the memory ends and fantasy begins.

* Memory: At night, fighting. I won't spread my legs. He leaves. Safe, maybe for one more night.

* Memory: I am seven. I am sitting in my room drawing pictures, entertaining myself. Only my dad is home. He comes in looking angry and mean. I see in his face a realization of an opportunity to play his secret game. He charges at me, grabs me by the back of the neck—I feel the pain now—and he shoves my face into his crotch and holds me there. He has on only underpants and he has an erection. Still holding me, he takes my pants off and he strips. He lies on his back and slides me up and down on his cock. At first I am aware of a strange sexual sensation, but that is replaced quickly by an intense feeling of wrongness and shame. I fight back and he punches me hard in the stomach. I remember, then, lying in bed, my hands holding my knees to my stomach, intense pain spreading from my ovaries through my entire insides. The memory renews the physical pain.

* Memory: I can't breathe. Then silence. It's cold. It's winter. I'm small. It's a dark Wisconsin night. I'm locked outside. Mom's face is contorted in crazy rage. She glares from inside the kitchen window at me, threatening to keep me outside in the cold till the lesson is learned . . .

I tried over and over to tell her what he was doing to me. But, mom insisted I was lying. I was dirty. I was eight and a slut—a tramp. I should never say those bad things about my dad again, she said.

(I can't go to work. I have a raging fever for three days. And then my body lets me see the past again.)

* Memory: My body is hot. I'm burning up. The image of an open oven door appears and a hand pushes me toward the heat. "Stop lying. God will punish you! You make up lies about him again and I will put you in that oven. Apologize to your dad."

I go down the stairs where dad stokes the coal furnace in the basement. He is angry. "You are not to tell about our secret games.

173

No one will ever believe you. Are you trying to break up the family?" Another hand pushes me toward the fire, the heat. "I'll throw you in the furnace if you keep telling lies!"

\* Memory: Too much pain and I tell her again.

\* Memory: I can't breathe. There is a pillow on my face. He won't let me breathe! He won't let me scream! I can't fight back . . . I wake up in the morning, eleven years old, three years before menstruation. I'm bleeding. I walk downstairs, scared to tell my mom. She has never told me about bleeding and I don't know what is happening to me. She reacts with surprise and seems upset. Not knowing I'm torn and not bleeding as a woman, she sends me to the bathroom and I hear unclear words she has with dad. The rapes stop. She doesn't want a pregnant eleven-year-old daughter.

\* Memory: Mom tells me to get in the bathtub. She says I'm filthy. It's too hot—really too hot. "Don't make me get in there!" She is stronger, and my skin scalds and turns lobster red, burning.

\* Memory: More water. She knows what I said is true, but she sees me as dirt, not what he has done as dirty. I'm in the bathtub again. She scrubs with a hard brush. Her face is changing and she becomes a monster, losing control, her scrubbing intensifies and then she is holding me and pushing me under the water. I know she is trying to kill me and at first I feel a passive submission. But inside I begin to grow. I'm getting larger and suddenly I'm fighting with all my strength. I feel larger and larger. Larger than she is. I survive.

(Perhaps I decided then to grow as heavy and large as I must to protect myself, to defend my life.)

\* Memory: Water. I feel her hand on my chest, pushing. Her face is filled with hate and she makes no sound. She seems crazy and has chosen this time to blot out the flaw in her picture of the oh-so-perfect family. With little struggle she overpowers me. I leave my body and the memory turns to fearful blackness. At a later time my memory clears and I see the rest of the scene as if I am a spectator with a camera viewing from beneath the water. The image is split, clear on top and blurred on the bottom. I see mom. She has changed her mind and grabs the drowning child by her hair, hauling her

174

from beneath the water. The child's eyes are glassy, almost lifeless. She is limp and very quiet.

**** 

When I was eleven, I knew I needed help. My life was not safe. Remembering now, I feel desperately lost. I want attention. I want someone to notice my hurt and my wounds. But they are inside me and no one sees. What to do? I remember. I walk in the hills. I bang my face and my head on rocks. My lips bleed. I will return and my hurt will be seen. Maybe someone will take care. Maybe someone will attend. Maybe the nightmare will end. I want someone to care. I want to be safe.

Soon after this walk the incest stopped. We moved to a different house and I shared a room with my sister. However, my mother always watched me and required me to work for her. I took care of the younger children. I cleaned. I cooked. When I was eleven, I was sent to work in the vast truck gardens near where we lived. During the summer this took ten hours a day, six days a week. My pay went to my mom. In exchange, she sewed me clothes. She made them ugly to make me look ugly and unappealing. Later, after moving to the new house where I shared a room, gaining protection, I was allowed to keep some of the money and had only to pay weekly rent to her. I was the only child, out of six, required to pay rent.

**** 

Sometimes I feel like a piece of broken glass on an ocean floor, waves of feelings rolling over me for many years. Now I've discovered how finely polished I am becoming, ready to wash up on shore and be seen.

I started psychotherapy because:

1. I hated mom and was never close to the family. I didn't know why.

2. I had abused drugs (pot, coke, qualudes, speed, etc.) and I was ready to stop.

3. I loved a woman (though she didn't know) and I didn't know what to do about my feelings.

I learned that my fear of people, my distaste bordering on terror when I heard loud yelling, and my lack of social skills all stemmed from the craziness ing my family. I told my therapist, the first time I saw her, "I just had a normal, ordinary, happy childhood." I had a hard time believing myself and believing in myself. I have kept my pain buried so deep that when it begins to emerge, I have a difficult time. The feelings tend to get stuck. I have never had practice feeling. I have worked for one-and-a-half years and I still have doubts that this horror happened.

I maintain some loyalty to my parents. Betraying them and their words is hard. It makes me feel lost, empty and without roots. I work with affirmations to reinforce my strength and replace my family's words of shame. Sometimes I blame my past when I can't relate to people in the present or even be with people. I don't reach out. I feel disliked and repulsive. I'm at a loss for words. Sometimes I feel hopeless. It is taking too long. Nothing is really changing, it seems. It's all too painful.

Sometimes when I hear another woman's story I begin to relive my own, over and over. It's so hard.

\* \* \* \*

\* Dream: My parents watch me carefully. We are at a dance and everyone else plays and enjoys. I begin to bob to the music and they tell me to stop. I try again, and again. Finally I ignore their commands. They may try, but the rhythm and vitality of my life will not be stopped. But, I fall off the chair only realizing then that I am a little girl and I have no face, no arms, no feet.

\* Dream: I'm driving to my house in a snowstorm. I don't know why, but I feel concerned and worried. It is important I get there soon. Arriving, I notice there are no footprints in the snow and no one is inside caring for the little girl there. I enter and colors are gone. My vision tunnels and all I see is black and white. The little girl walks into the scope on my vision and I ask her what she is doing here. She says she is waiting for me to take care of her. I feel deeply sad that I have not been there for her before. She is older now. She has arms and legs. She has learned she can walk. Her clothes are too big and hang on her. A hooded parka covers her facelessness.

* Dream: I am with this girl again, but she has grown into her clothes and is in her teens. She takes me through her house and I see that between each room there is an empty space like a musty, dusty unfinished closet. Again, there is an absence of color: all black and white and empty feeling. The rooms adjoining, however, contrast with blandly colored decor. The girl indicates that I am to go upstairs by myself, and I do. I walk into my old room. I look out the window and see her on a swing. She smiles at me and sails high against a blue sky. Now I know it's going to be all right. I know she is the same as the others in previous dreams. I know there is change.

* Dream: Every night throughout one week I am at war with my family. They try in many different ways to capture and control me. They are long dreams, tiring, with constant battles and close escapes. My family—the enemy—takes my therapist and holds her, threatening to hurt her if I don't give up. I pretend to give myself in trade for her, but we outwit them and the two of us run to freedom. They admit defeat.

* Dream: Ocean waves. Peaceful watching changes to a realization that a tidal wave is forming. My family is on the beach and I try to yell warnings. They ignore me. They don't notice the danger and I seek shelter and high ground, finding a glass-walled building, a safe observation point. I watch the giant wave, feeling sad, yet relieved as my family is washed away and drowned.

* Dream: I'm playing golf where many crocodile-filled streams flow through the greens. I have no problem crossing the water. The reptiles are my friends. I see frightened sheep on the hill nearby and I know they need care, need to be tended and moved to a different location where they will be safe and well-fed. I forget golf and go to them. They sense my feelings and energy. The sheep follow me down the hill and we cross the streams. The crocodiles do not cooperate and I have to take the sheep one-at-a-time to safety. I lose one and one gets injured. However, I feel satisfied and accomplished. I did what had to be done to save them.

* Dream: Four young girls in a room are required, by a woman I know is my mother, to weigh in their pillows every night. The weight determines how much they should be charged to stay. The

oldest girl and I are going to leave soon. We are very close and I feel sad she is leaving before me. My mother is in a hateful mood because the girl is leaving. She hates me and makes me pay for two pillows the night the girl is to leave. Now I have no more money and it costs to leave. I feel trapped, angry and sad, but I am not allowed to speak my feelings. The woman is pleased with my pain. I decide I will leave soon anyway. I feel happy and know I have made a good decision. The older girl sleeps on a mattress inside the wall. I sleep on the bed and our heads are close together. She says we can meet when I get out and she wants me to get out as soon as I can. Then, she prepares to leave and I feel sad and disgusted. The woman, with no feeling, hugs the girl goodbye. The woman seems meaner to me now, but kinder to the other girls. With my friend gone, the woman feels more in control. I decided to leave immediately. I say goodbye to the younger girls, hug the woman goodbye, aware of feeling I never belonged here. Leaving, I know I am free of ugliness and I can feel my power and happiness deep inside me.

\* \* \* \*

The work I am doing is the hardest I have ever done. I am often overwhelmed. Sometimes I feel very small and see my hands as if they were a child's. Or I look down and my legs have become very small and short.

I have a seven-year-old friend named Missy, whom I have known since birth. Sometimes when I touch her I feel like my father touching me and I feel the touches on my body and I am disgusted and afraid. I have trouble coping with my confusion when the past creeps into the present.

In the therapy room, two pillows become my parents. I tell them, "You hurt me! You caused me pain and you robbed me of my childhood and my life." I tell them over and over what they did to me and my spoken words become the truth that drowns their lies.

One day I sculpted two lead figures—my parents. I placed rocks in their stomachs and carefully wrapped their arms around to hold the rocks in place. I took them to a nearby reservoir and I told them: "The rocks are your burden to carry forever as you made me carry mine." I throw them into the deep water and say: "You can sink or swim like I had to."

Another time I took their picture and burned it. The flames

consumed them as my rage consumes me. But my rage also releases me.

I brought a doll to take care of so I could learn to take better care of myself. For weeks "Hannah" lay on my bed and I looked at her and heard in my head the same abusive words my parents spoke to me. "Look at her lying there, just asking for it. She really deserves what she gets." "Slut!"

I couldn't touch her without feeling painful touches on me. Then, gradually, I began to speak gentle, caring words to her—words that should have been spoken to me. I can even hold her now and I feel no shame with her. I even introduce Hannah to my other friends!

I write my story hoping it will be published and read.

My fantasy: I want my parents to know what they did to me, so I send them a published copy. They would read my story and then acknowledge what they did.

In reality, I'm afraid they would still deny the incest and abuse. I'm afraid they would once again say, "You are bad and just trying to break up our family again."

For now, I go on with my painful work. I'm in the middle of it and memories emerge and startle me with the cruelty and hate I was forced to live through. I have a supportive, caring therapist and she reassures me and cares for me. A small part of me is learning to take over for her and to support and love myself. I move emotionally from reliving a nightmare to experiencing clarity and power in my life. I marvel at the strength I must have—to have lived through my childhood. I AM A SURVIVOR.


**C. J. Mileski:** A special thanks to my therapist Dr. Molly Gierasch for helping me to write my story. Her support and support from friends made my story truly a healing process.

# Letter to Mother

1/12/85

dear mother,

i am finally able to write to you with a little bit of what is going on for me. you were absolutely correct when you said that my anger with you on the phone that night was out of proportion to my concern. some of my anger came from the issues discussed in the enclosed article concerning role models. but still, that wasn't quite it. so i decided not to contact you again until i could figure out what was really going on. and lo and behold i did it. surprise surprise i am finally able to be angry, furious, outraged, with you about your part in my childhood as an incest victim of five, count them mother, five men. dear daddy, dear uncle jack, the internist you dragged me to every year for a physical, the doctor dear daddy dragged me to for the nasty little mole on my ass that so fascinated the two of them along with other parts of me (note four doctors, those glorious men of healing) and of course the neighbor boy david. so what i have been doing is remembering. a lot. and the memories are crazy making and sad and my memories include all the times, and there were many, that i begged you, pleaded with you, screamed at you, not to leave me alone, not to make me go see that doctor, not to make me live with "that man" any more. (or was that all in my mind because i knew talking with you was useless.)

when i was four years old and harold left you and you lay on that bed and cried i vowed to take care of you and protect you and, if it was in my power, you would never cry again. when dear daddy told me that to tell you of his doings would make you cry—there was no question in my mind that you would never know about how he would make me jerk him off and then make me stand there, silently, alone, while he smeared his come in my face (one of the many, many sadistic sick things he would do—in your bedroom). no question in my mind that my pain was nothing compared to your pain. where did i learn that i had to be there for you, because you certainly were not there for me (i can remember being scared of going to sleep in a bed because i knew if i fell there would be no one there to catch me) and you certainly could not take care of yourself. and when he would corner me in the family room and beat me with his belt buckle, i would watch you whimper in the corner of the room, begging him to stop, but never just taking me in your arms and protecting me from anything. and when he would command that no one could talk to me until i would break to his whims, you obeyed him and left me isolated and freaked out. and when i came home from europe from one month of living hell from his hands and mouth and penis never leaving my 5th grade body alone and cried and begged you to leave him and and and. i feel like i could go on forever.

and maybe i should go on forever. maybe i should tell you every detail. i just don't know if that's what it would take. and take for what? for me to excuse you. for me to rationalize again your desertion of me and two other little girls.

new year's eve when i lay there and finally for the first time spoke out loud to my self and remembered more and more, i wanted at that moment to ask you three questions. but i didn't want and still do not want an answer from you.

1. where were you?
2. why did you (how could you) sell me (us) down the river so easily?
3. why did i take care of you all those years when the sacrifices that we made for each other were so one sided. me a child and you supposedly the adult to protect me from harm, humiliation, violation, etc. etc.

i am very, very angry with you.

i will not hurry this process in any way.

it is clear to me—at 33—that this work, this fun, exciting, thought-provoking, relationship-encouraging, incest work, will be with me as long as i live.

i will never be free of it. and if i am never free of my anger for you and for any concerned, sensitive, caring, protecting adult like you that is okay by me.

i don't want to hear you trivialize my pain ever again by telling me that it was so long ago, that you had a hard childhood also, that there is really no reason to detest you for this because you are such a good person now.

this anger may be a phase—but my realizations about your lack of responsibility towards me and your betrayal of me and your burden on us as an ineffective, out of touch, unloving, abusive parent is not a phase.

my two younger sisters have been in touch with their anger with you for a long time. the fact that it took me this long to stop making excuses for you is something to think about.

and i suggest you do think about this and take this seriously. as seriously as i must to live with my memories and loss and my inability to trust any human being on this earth and the knowledge that everyone betrays you and if someone says they love you, you can expect to pay sexually, and can expect to protect them and get nothing in return. and you dear mother helped me to learn all of this.

please don't even think of writing or calling me.


**Anna Ace:** This letter speaks of very personal events in my life. So personal that I have not even shown this to some of my closest friends. But I'm glad I wrote it. I hope, for all of us who have experienced this, that the lessons don't get lost in the pain.

# I Understand Ronald Reagan
# Because I Understand My Father

I understand Ronald Reagan
    because I understand my father.

My father thinks that his family is an
    extension of him
Just like Ronald Reagan thinks the world is an
    extension of the United States.
My father, the head, must run the family.
That is the logic, like the President runs the
country.
Congress, family meetings, are student
    councils—you listen to them attentively
    and then go right on and do what you planned
    to do.
        If you are my father.
        Or Ronald Reagan.
You are a moral man.
    You have a strong code of personal ethics.
        You are deeply wounded if someone
            questions your moral integrity.
There is one code of ethics
and you are it.
You are the head
    and you, father, know what's best.
Your mentor/model
    is omnipotent
        omnipresent
        omniscient
Any questioning of your truth is
    insurrection
    treason
    heresy

There is but One Truth
        One God
        One Nation Indivisible
Every country must have one leader
    Every family one head
If not,
    dissension
    anarchy
    chaos
        (freedom)
There is no disagreement
There can be no disagreement
With one truth
    from one source
There is only
    heresy:
Thou shalt have no other Gods above me
    treason:
My country right or wrong
    insurrection:
How dare you talk back to me.


I know why Ronald Reagan believed he had the
    right to invade Grenada
Because I understand why my father
    believed he had the right to invade me.
There was no invasion, he believed.
It hurts me to hear you say that, he says.
I don't understand how you can say that.
I did it for your own good.
I did it because I love you.
I did it for good and noble reasons
because I am a good and noble person.


I know what's best for Grenada.
I know better than the Grenadians
    what's best for them.
I am doing this for your own good.
I am hurting you for your own good.
Someday you will thank me.

I am teaching you.
I am helping you.
I am a kind person.
I am doing this out of kindness.

My father has never called me by my name.
Sometimes he calls me by my
   mother's name, often by my sister's
   occasionally by my daughter's.
He has one son.  He always gets his
name right.  It is the same as his
own name.  He has two grandsons.  He
always gets their names right.  One of
them is named after him.

When Ronald Reagan was Governor of California, he authorized
the wholesale cutting-down of
Redwoods, thousands of years old,
the oldest living creatures on earth—
and he said, "You've seen one Redwood,
you've seen them all."

My father has never gone camping
or hiking.  He rides horses.
He breaks them first.  One time I
watched him work with a
horse whose hind leg he'd tied to the
opposite front leg.  He came behind the
horse and hit him on the rump with
a blanket.  When the horse tried
to kick, he fell over.  For hours it
went on, hit and kick and fall and I
cried and begged him to stop, he
was hurting the horse.  He laughed
and said, "He has to hurt to learn he
can't kick."  By noon the horse
stood still when it was hit on the rump
with a blanket.
My son was three years old and he
sucked his thumb and one Saturday morning

185

after breakfast his father decided
to break him of the habit. He
made David sit at the table while
he called him a sissy and a baby and said
only babies suck their thumbs. When
David cried he called him a baby all
the harder. I asked him to stop.
"He's not going to stop any other way,"
my husband responded. By noon David
had stopped crying and had promised
he would never suck his thumb again.

Ronald Reagan had to teach the Cubans a lesson.
There was only one way
they would learn.
He taught them in Grenada.

When my father was a boy he
had a horse who he named and
he still remembers that horse's
name. One day he came home and
his horse was gone. His father had
sold some horses to buy a car. My
father's horse was one of them.
My father cried and cried. He was
heartbroken. One day he saw his
horse in a neighboring field. He
cut through the fence and brought his
horse home. His father made him
take the horse back. "Weren't
you angry?" I asked my father.
"No. My father did what was
right," he said.

My father is a sensitive man.
He cried at his 50th wedding
anniversary and my mother didn't.
He is a kind man.
When I came out of the lake last
summer he brought me warm

water to wash my feet before I went
into the house.

My father incested me when I was
  five.
He beat my sister once until the
  blood spurted out of her elbow.
He beat my brother once for talking
  back.
He raped my mother once while
  I was lying sick beside their bed.
My father is a banker.
A regional officer in the church.
One of the most respected men in
  his community.
My father voted for Ronald Reagan and
  will again in the next election.


**Sara Wylie:** My father was the age I am now when he violated me.
People thought he was in his prime then: middle-aged, handsome,
successful and respected. Now he's old and nobody needs him.
He's in the way. He can no longer order the world. He's learning
powerlessness, and he's doing it quite gracefully. I think he's in his
prime. We talk now about things that are important to us, and he
respects my opinions. After a recent discussion he agreed to write
letters opposing Reagan's intervention in Central America.

# Dear Mom

*You shall know
the truth
and the truth
shall set you free*


Dear Mom,

You have said that I've been a lousy mother because your mother died when you were 10 years old. You were so well brainwashed by the patriarchy that you blame the female too—but it wasn't you or me or your mother—it was the males who committed the crimes. I don't know if your father molested you. I only know there was a good possibility. He raised you alone from age 10 on. He raised you alone in that house right next door to the house where Uncle Harold raped and molested me over a period of 3-4 years, beginning when I was around 10. Incredible? I once thought so too. I detached it all from my memory because it was so incredible. When I was a child and told you—you told me: "Oh, Uncle Harold would never do a thing like that!" Now you deny that I ever told you. Read *Conspiracy of Silence* Mom, and Mom since you're almost 70 years old, it's very hard to say all this—something in me wants to keep on protecting you in your beautiful WASP world—you the minister's wife—you the theological seminary professor's wife.[1] How do I tell you what your father did to me on the walks in the woods behind our house in Absecon when I was 3-4-5 years old. *How* do I tell you? You who made me take those walks. Did you know? Can you ever face the truth of my experience? Face the truth of what may have been your experience too only your mind has blocked it because it's too intensely painful—my mind did! And now I know why all those years all I ever really wanted to do was die. I'm 47 years old and I only began remembering last year . . . and now I know why and how I've been all those years—depressed—scared to death of tons of situations—none of it made any sense 'til now. It's time to quit blaming

188

ourselves as women. It's time to hold the perpetrators responsible for their crimes—yes, crimes, Mom.

All I consciously remembered for years was Uncle Harold picking me up with his hand between my legs and carrying me into his house from his side porch. Only last summer did I remember what he did to me inside that house. Do you want to know Mom? Why don't you ever ask? Oh, of course, he would never do a thing like that—so I must be crazy—it was real crazy making Mom, not being believed about the most awful experience of my life and now the devastation continues as I still sense your disbelief. How will you ever be able to hear when I try to tell you about Daddy crawling into bed with me when I was 11—biologically a woman then—and you were pregnant, down the hall in another bedroom. His choice—his choice—not your fault, not mine, Mom. You and the church taught me to be faithful to one man, a bit confusing when deep inside I was learning that it was OK for two pillars of the church to get their kicks off my body—one one day—one the next.

One of my recurring nightmares is of being around 10—naked from the waist down—wrapped from the waist up in men's coats— my head covered by the coats so I can't see the men, can't scream and I'm being rammed upside down between the altar rails and the organ in that last church Daddy served just one block from Uncle Harold's house . . . I relive the wooden feel and smell of that altar and those woollen coats in every nightmare. It's semi-dark, someone spreads my legs while I'm upside down—then I wake up. It probably never happened Mom but oh good grief how symbolic of what the patriarchy did to me. I was well trained. Every time I said no to an elder or questioned any authority, I got spanked. I learned my lesson well, Mom—just don't ever complain or say no or you'll get hurt. I'm surprised I'm still alive—that I didn't kill myself all those times I wanted to die. You and the church taught me to forgive and forget. I can forgive, Mom, but I will never forget, Mom, never.


P.S. So you'll probably say I've made this all up or that I've exaggerated. Do you want to hear what Uncle Harold did to me inside his house—or some other things about Daddy? This is only the tip of the iceberg, Mom. This is my truth, my experience. This is no exaggeration. This is me, your only daughter, and what my life was really like.

**Beth-Luis-Nion**

[1] Sandra Butler, *Conspiracy of Silence: The Trauma of Incest* (San Francisco: New Glide Publications, 1978).

# Speaking Out as a Survivor

Almost exactly two years ago tonight, I had just left a meeting at the YW with my friend Mayda. It was 9:00, the first really warm evening of the spring. The night air, the stars drew us. We decided to walk the three blocks to my house along University Boulevard, rather than riding with some other friends. We agreed to meet them at my house.

As we walked, we talked and laughed. About halfway home a man passed us, running. I didn't think much about it. When we were just around the corner from my house, a man standing in a dark, shady yard called out to us: "Stop right there." It didn't register at first. "I said STOP." We looked up. The man was pointing a long-barreled handgun at our heads, standing in an "executioner's" pose, about three feet away. I said, "OK, we stopped," irritated, not yet scared.

I figured he was going to rob us. I only had a few dollars—big deal. And he'd have to work fast; this was a busy street. Somebody, riding by on a bike or walking home from the U or jogging, would see us. But nobody did.

"Don't look at my face. Get over here." He told Mayda to kneel down and put her head down. That seemed weird, but I still thought it was a robbery. He stood behind me. "How much money do you have?" "About five dollars, I think." "Give it to me." He sounded nervous. I handed him my wallet, but he told me to take out the money and give it to him. Yep, it's a robbery. He only wants money. This is almost over. But it wasn't.

He told Mayda to stay where she was. If she moved or yelled, he would kill me. He grabbed me by one arm, staying just behind me, pointing the gun at my neck, and told me to walk. And then I knew it wasn't just a robbery. But somehow I still didn't believe he could pull off anything more. He pushed me down the street, right under a street light, right past my own house. Where were the cars? Where were the usual bike riders and joggers? The neighborhood seemed deadly quiet. This had to be a bad dream. My friends were right inside the house, waiting for me with my housemate.

He pushed me into a dark alley, about a block from my home. Behind someone else's home—I don't know if they ever found out what happened that night by their back gate. I still remember the wire fence covered with shreds of an old parachute. I remember Mayda roaring, knew she was running to tell the others. Thanks to her, it was over very fast. The man ran off, leaving me lying in the gravel.

I heard the police helicopter. Its searchlight shone directly on me as I ran from the alley, clutching my shirt closed. Only seconds too late. I still couldn't believe it.

Two days later an *Arizona Daily Star* reporter put our case and that of nineteen other women (who knows how many more) together and got the police to admit that they thought the same man had raped us all in the previous nine months in the West University Neighborhood. Mayda and I had been sitting ducks. They had nicknamed him the Brazen Rapist. Brazen. A pathetic, angry, shaky, lucky, only semi-clever jerk.

My first reaction was fury. Later, I was terrified. I stared out my front door window at the street, stared wide-eyed at the ceiling in the dark when I heard the helicopter overhead, every night. "He" was out there. My chest was in a vice. I couldn't cry. I was too pissed off. I couldn't sleep. I wanted to stay alert; in case he pulled somebody behind *my* house, I would be there to stop him.

As the days went by, I started feeling stupid. How could I have been so dumb as to stop? Why was I so paralyzed by the gun? How could a jerk like that get *me*? I played the tape of the rape over and over again, thinking what I could have done differently. But generally, I let myself off the hook. Luckily, I knew about the blame-the-victim myth and refused to do that to myself. Luckily, I had supportive friends and family. I had permission to stay pissed off. I wanted to do something.

Then a group got together to organize the neighborhood, to warn women about the rapist and to design a strategy to stop him. We had a large neighborhood gathering at the Y. I started picking up on the questions that were circulating in the neighborhood: How big were these women? Why did they "submit" to the rapist? Why should we be scared to walk in the neighborhood—we don't have to put out the kind of "energy" that attracts a rapist. And I realized that for many people I was to blame for being raped. It would never happen to *them*. To this day it is hearing this myth, over and over, rather than the memory of the rape, which hurts and enrages me the most.

Before I was raped, I was a political woman. I was 35 years old. I had worked with battered women and abused children and poor people. I worked to end war. But all the time I was looking at reality through a foggy window, thinking I understood the extent of "social problems" and the difficulty of "solving" them. And once in a while, when I was faced with somebody else's crisis or my own bouts with depression, I would take my finger and rub a little "peep hole" in the window and look through it at the depth of pain that can exist in one human life. And I had some idea that if this pain were multiplied by millions I would have the totality of suffering in all human lives.

Being raped was like having someone smash that window for good. I finally understood that every rape statistic is a real woman and that woman is just like me. And every one of these women, like me, has a story. I understood that at the heart of our society is a hatred for women so strong that even women are infected by it. The "shame" of speaking out about rape stems from a deeply entrenched and constantly reinforced belief that we are to blame for our own victimization.

My own response, my way of dealing with my anger about this, is to work to end that hatred. It is no liberal knee-jerk reaction. It's for me, and for all those women like me whose bodies are debased on highway billboards, in cars parked in the desert, in city alleyways, homes, porn shops and theaters.

No one can tell me that my politics are the hysterical overreaction of a paranoid rape victim who has been pushed over the edge by a bad experience. I see reality. I have no distance from it, no more rationalizations to protect me. And I don't expect all of you to look at it tonight. I expect you to protect yourselves from our stories, as I did before with my foggy window. But please value us, the survivors, because we have looked through that window and we have seen the scary truth about our world, and we will let you know when the terror is over. We will feel it when that knot within us loosens and we know that we are finally safe in a world that really loves women and children.

**Peggy L. Placier:** I grew up in a very small town in the hills of southern Ohio. In many ways, I am still a shy, rural, working class person who has to force herself to speak in big groups. This text was my part of an eleven-woman Survivor Speak-Out. It was the first time I had made a public statement about my personal aftermath.

About the "politics of rape" I have been very outspoken. But many people get the idea that "political women" are preoccupied with analysis, with issues, with relationships between classes of people rather than personal feelings and relationships. We've certainly had to learn to operate in these more impersonal realms. But our commitment comes from the actual experience of oppression.

Explaining, through my speech, why transforming this society is a personal, lifelong commitment means a great deal to me. Thanks to the Speak-Out and to my experience with the women of Take Back The Night, I have found the support to speak up for what I believe.

# Journal Entries

December 18—I had another bout with the monster. I always think he is dead, but he is asleep. It is the faces I have dreams about, dreams like death. They are concave. They look toward the inside of the bodies, not the out, and the eyes are completely white because the black pupils are inside, always pointed inward. And I'm there, and I can't speak, and I can't be quiet. This is my part.

The dreams terrify me as much as they did before. But in a different way. Before, especially at first, I was frightened by the prospect of going over to the other side, being crazy. This time it is simply frightening to learn it's still there. Because it's been *years* now, two, almost three. Three in January.

It is always this feeling of having been defeated.

January—How is it that a life so carefully built can be so fragile? I hate myself for being afraid. Can't stay where I am, but curse myself for going backward. Does anyone else know this? What it feels like to *know* strength, because it used to be there, but *feel* nothing but weak. To feel panic fill you up like water.

January 20—This picture of myself. What am I trying to build? In my small, cold house when I light my little fireplace each night and fearfully, bravely, proudly sleep alone? I am kidding myself. I don't sleep.

February—I can't manage anything. It's Friday afternoon, and I can't stand being in the house—I'm too scared. Has that bastard stolen Friday afternoons from me forever? I want to put him on trial, demand from him retribution for all the things he has stolen from me.

February—The sky is made of lead and so low I can't straighten up. There are holes in the lead, and sometimes the sun comes through, but that's an accident.

I have always felt this way. When my father told me about

menstruation. That a woman couldn't be president, because suppose there was a war and she was on her period. I hadn't even begun to menstruate, and already it was this way.

March 14—I read some poems by a Florence inmate, convicted of rape for the third time:
> Why should I be guilty
> for the simple brains that I fried?
> For getting over another's mind?
> If it was weak,
> I was able to penetrate it.
> I shouldn't be accountable for that.

I think I understood rape, from his point of view, for the first time when I read this. The philosophy of "might makes right," that the power to threaten and even destroy another person is *good*, and that this power—just by virtue of its existence—confers on its owner the right to use it. The power's the thing. If you have the bomb, why not drop it on Hiroshima?

No wonder there is so much rape in this country.

March 21—When it comes back, it comes so hard. Watching *Hearts and Minds*, the Vietnamese woman hysterical with grief, crawling into the grave with her son. And Westmoreland saying (precisely): "The Oriental doesn't place the same value on life that we do. In the philosophy of the Oriental, life is cheap."[1]

On the walk home, it enraged me to see the calm houses lit up, the people inside eating dinner.

March 24—What a confusion of morality. I read that a quarter of all veterans who came back from heavy combat in Vietnam have been arrested on criminal charges. Some are rapists, no doubt. Before, they dropped napalm on children, ripped open women's heads with their bombs. And got medals.

March 25—A line from D.H. Lawrence's *The Fox*: "You truly know a thing by killing it."[2] Have I been truly known, and killed? HE DIDN'T KNOW ME. DID NOT SEE MY BRAIN, EVEN IF HE FRIED IT. DIDN'T LOOK IN THE SKILLET WHILE IT COOKED. Like the dream-face, he was too busy looking inward.

*Can I kill it?* By understanding? By writing poems, scribbling in a journal?

March 28—Audre Lorde writes about her radical mastectomy in *The Cancer Journals*. Her decision against wearing a prosthesis—"the fantasy of reconstruction." No one would ever insist that Moshe Dayan wear a glass eye. She takes comfort from the Dahome warriors of the Amazon, who had their right breasts amputated in order to be better archers.

But Audre, I don't know how to make use of my loss. I'm not sure I can shoot straighter for it.

March 29—I'm laboring over poetry, nervous about the reading. How can I possibly do this well? It's the moral I want to tell, *scream*, not the story. But that won't do. Over and over I make myself breathe slowly, like the cops did. Just tell the story. If it's the right one, if it's clear, the moral will follow. I am only working towards a journalism of the emotions.

But even to tell a story, you have to trust.

April—I read the rape poem, at a women's poetry reading. I admitted that it would take courage, and then I read it, and then it was done. So many women hugged me, thanked me, after. Especially for "Ten Forty-Four" they said.

Just before I left, a man—I don't know his name—told me he had never had to think about it that way before. He gave me this note, sort of a poem:

I listened to a poet tonight
She touched me with a gentle sadness

Words are so pitifully inadequate
Our souls cry
Our spirit's flight
Who will hear?

Beyond my understanding,
the woman's sadness.
I will still try.

197

I thought: I have lived long enough to do something important in this world.

April 23—Last night I was alone, and slept well, with no lights on.

**Barbara Kingsolver**

[1] Peter Davis, director, *Hearts and Minds*, Warner Brothers, 1974.
[2] D. H. Lawrence, *The Fox* (New York: Viking Press, 1923).

# Help Is Available

## Local and National Resources

At this point, many of you may be asking where do you go from here, where do you get some help, find people who will understand what has happened to you. Ten years ago, finding help would have been difficult. Today numerous programs, both nationally and locally based, provide help, support, therapy and shelter for survivors of sexual abuse nationwide. What follows is a resource guide to programs, rape crisis centers, hot lines, child protective services and other agencies that work with the treatment and prevention of child sexual abuse, rape, molest, incest and other forms of sexual victimization.

Rape Crisis Centers exist in most states and many cities. Typically non-profit agencies trained to work with rape survivors and many rape crisis centers are staffed primarily by female volunteers and professional counselors. Rape crisis centers usually provide crisis intervention for victims and their families. Support and advocacy are available to assist victims through the medical examination, police investigation and court process. Many rape crisis centers also have hot-line numbers and provide help on a 24-hour basis. Prevention and education programs are another primary function of rape centers. Many centers have a speakers' bureau to address rape issues in the community. For local listings, check the Emergency Numbers page (usually the first page in your telephone directory), look in your local Yellow Pages telephone directory under "Social Service Organizations" and "Human Service Organizations," or contact The National Coalition Against Sexual Assault (see next paragraph).

Two national organizations have been established to combat rape. The first is the National Coalition Against Sexual Assault (NCASA). Staffed by volunteers from every state, NCASA is an organization designed to encourage networking, communication and skill sharing between organizations and individuals that work with rape victims. They will share their up-to-date listings of the rape crisis centers across the country with anyone upon request. Their address is Judith Condo; NCASA; Albany County Rape Crisis Center; Room 1100; 112 State Street; Albany, NY 12207. Their phone number is (518) 447-7100.

Another national organization set up to support rape victims is the National Center for the Prevention and Control of Rape (NCPCR). Typically, they fund research and other projects involving rape counseling, prevention and education. Individuals and organizations that are interested in research can contact NCPCR at NCPCR, Division of Special Mental Health Programs; National Institute of Mental Health; Room 6C12; 5600 Fishers Lane; Rockville, MD 20857. The phone number is (301) 443-1910.

The National Organization for Victim Assistance (NOVA) is a private, non-profit organization of victim and witness assistance practitioners, criminal justice professionals, researchers, former victims and others committed to the recognition of victim rights. In most cities and states, the county attorney's office has a Victim Witness Assistance Program. These programs work with victim restitution, compensation, counseling, advocacy as well as medical and legal needs. To contact NOVA for your local chapter, write or call NOVA; 717 D Street, N.W.; Washington, D.C. 20004; (202) 393-NOVA.

First started in 1971, Child Sexual Abuse Treatment Programs (CSATP) were designed as self-help programs for incestuous families. Parents United, Adults Molested as Children, and Daughters and Sons United are the self-help components of CSATP. Individual and peer-group counseling is the main focus of CSATP programs. Perpetrators and their partners, as well as victims, can receive help through this organization. The national chapter can help you contact your local chapter at Child Abuse Treatment Program; Parents United; P.O. Box 952; San Jose, CA 95108; (408) 280-5055.

The Child Assault Prevention Project (CAP) is a prevention and education project for children and adults. The project offers classroom workshops using a combination of role playing and guided group discussions which train children to recognize and deal with potentially dangerous situations. CAP programs originated in the state of Ohio and now are established in communities throughout the country. To obtain more information about CAP projects, contact Child Assault Prevention Project; Women Against Rape; P.O. Box 02084; Columbus, OH 43202; (614) 291-9751.

Victims of Incest Can Emerge Survivors (VOICES) is a national network that helps victims to empower themselves to become survivors and works to prevent child sexual abuse. VOICES has initiated self-help groups for victims nationwide and offers a referral service to help victims throughout America find therapists, agencies or existing self-help groups which they can attend. For more information on your local chapter, contact VOICES, INC.; P.O. Box 148309; Chicago, IL 60614.

*Response, To the Victimization of Women and Children* is a journal published by the Center for Women Policy Studies (CWPS). CWPS is a non-profit, policy-research organization that conducts research and develops information on a variety of issues affecting women. If you are interested in reading about sexual assault and other issues affecting women, contact *Response*; Suite 508; 2000 P Street, N.W.; Washington, D.C. 20036.

Child Protective Service is the state-mandated agency designed to protect children and to investigate reports of sexual abuse, physical abuse, emotional abuse and the neglect of children. Typically, their services include investigation of child abuse reports, child abuse 24-hour hot lines, prevention and education programs, advocacy and support services for victims and their families. Check the Emergency Numbers page in the White Pages telephone directory under "Child Abuse Hotline" or check the city, state or government listings for local services.

The National Coalition Against Domestic Violence (NCADV) is an organization designed to encourage networking, communication and resource sharing between organizations and individuals that work with domestic violence. They will share their up-to-date listings of the domestic violence shelters across the country upon request. NCADV can be contacted at NCADV; Suite 306; 2401 Virginia Avenue, N.W.; Washington, D.C. 20037; (202) 293-8860.

The following are some useful 800 numbers:

**1-800-VICTIMS**
Crime Victims' Legal Resource Center
McGeorge School of Law

**1-800-424-7827**
National Sheriffs' Association Victim Assistance Program

**1-800-4-A-Child**
Childhelp USA's National Child Abuse Hotline

**1-800-843-5678**
The National Center for Missing and Exploited Children

**1-800-222-Find**
Department of Justice Missing Children Hotline

**1-800-237-2542**
Bureau of Missing Children Hotline

There are many people and organizations willing to help survivors of sexual assault. Community mental health centers, police departments, hospital emergency rooms, grass-roots political organizations (for example, Take Back The Night, National Organization of Women, and Gay Rights), religious groups, United Ways women's centers at university and college campuses and even civic organizations and clubs have become advocates in the area of sexual assault.

Reaching out for help is hard work and takes a lot of courage. Due to unstable funding, staff changes and the volunteer nature of many of the organizations listed above, do not be too discouraged if you have some difficulty contacting them. Also, do not give up if you reach out and the agency or individual responding is insensitive, impatient or not knowledgeable about your concerns. It is important to try another place or to ask to speak to a different person. Getting the right help means finding someone who has skills and knowledge in the area of sexual abuse, who has a nonjudgmental and empathetic attitude.

Although you may feel scared when acknowledging that you were victimized and that your sexual abuse experience(s) has impacted you and those around you, the freedom you can feel is really worth it. Joining a group or talking to a counselor or therapist about your experiences provides a safe environment to express your feelings. Therapy can help you feel less isolated, foster trust in yourself, build self-esteem, strengthen your decision-making and problem-solving skills and improve your interpersonal relationships. Most importantly, therapy can finally allow you to let go—let go of the pain, of the horror, humiliation, sadness, guilt, and begin to integrate the sexual abuse experience into your life.

Michele Gorcey, M.S.W.
San Diego, California

# About the Editors

**Pamela Portwood**, M.F.A., is a free-lance writer, art critic, poet and art critic. She writes a column on the visual arts for *Artspace: Southwestern Contemporary Arts Quarterly* and is the poetry editor for the *Clarion*, a Tucson-based women's newspaper. Her own poetry has appeared in various publications, including *Ikon*, *Primavera* and *Plexus*.

Currently, she is seeking a publisher for "Learning to Speak," a poetry manuscript about her process of working through and healing from the consequences of incest and rape in her life. As a feminist activist, she has read many of her incest poems in public and has spoken and written extensively about the issues of sexual violence.

\* \* \* \*

**Michele Gorcey**, M.S.W., specializes in working with adult survivors of incest, rape and child sexual abuse in her clinical practice. Previously, she founded and directed a long-term treatment program for rape and incest survivors at Kino Community Hospital in Tucson, Arizona. She has co-authored and published two articles on the research findings of a three-year study, which she coordinated, on the long-term effects of rape and incest.

As an activist in the anti-rape movement, she has served on the board of directors of the National Coalition Against Sexual Assault and of the Tucson Rape Crisis Center, on the advisory board of Arizona State University's School of Social Work, as co-founder of the Rape Task Force and the Coordinating Committee on Sexual and Domestic Violence (in Tucson). In 1984, she represented eight southwestern states at the National Symposium on Sexual Assault sponsored by the F.B.I. and the U.S. Attorney General's Office. Currently, she is a board member for the Sexual Assault Coordinating Council in San Diego, California. She has delivered addresses and workshops both locally and nationally on the issues of sexual assault.

**\* \* \* \***

**Peggy Sanders** lives with her husband, John, in Tucson, Arizona. Their professional work—collecting and managing database and graphic information for archaeological expeditions—takes them to such places as Cyprus and Iraq, in addition to domestic territories.

Besides archaeology-related endeavors, her interests include drawing and painting, particularly the human form. Her hope is to incorporate her diverse experiences and artistic talents into stories for young readers.

 **Mother Courage Press**

In addition to *Rebirth of Power*, Mother Courage Press publishes

*Why Me? Help for victims of child sexual abuse (even if they are adults now)* by Lynn B. Daugherty. This book was written to be read by survivors of child sexual abuse who are now teenagers or adults. It is also intended for counselors or other people who want to understand and help these survivors. It was chosen for the Editors Choice Award for Young Adults in 1986 by the American Library Association's publication, *booklist*. Its reviewer wrote, "Emphasizing the responsibility of the abuser, the fact that abuse is a widespread experience, and the dynamics of an abusive situation, Daugherty begins the process of healing psychological wounds."
Paperback, (112 pages) $7.95

*Something Happened to Me* by Phyllis Sweet. This is a sensitive, straight-forward book designed to help children victimized by incest or other sexual abuse. A reviewer for *Young Children, the Official Journal of the National Association for the Education of Young Children*, wrote, "The marvelous introduction and epilogue are written for adults and reveal the extraordinary care that the author, a school psychologist, has taken to assure the dignity and self-worth of children from troubled families."
Paperback, Illustrated, 8¹/2 by 11, (36 pages) $4.95

*Fear or Freedom, a Woman's Options in Social Survival and Physical Defense* by Susan E. Smith. *Library Journal* in its March 1, 1987 issue highly recommended *Fear or Freedom* and called it "an important new approach to self-defense for women." Using the results of a four-part research project on rape, assault and successful resistance stories involving 209 women and her nine years of study in the martial arts, the author has developed a strategy that involves situational advantages, interaction, inter-personal dynamics, attack styles and all degrees of confrontation. She shows why and how known-assailant rape is the most preventable and easiest to defend against. Women today need answers—not admonitions.

The book realistically offers options to fear of social intimidation and fear of violent crime.
Paperback, Illustrated, $8^1/2$ by 11, (224 pages) $11.95

Watch for more healing and helping books, novels, biographies and poetry with a feminist perspective from Mother Courage Press.

If you don't find them in your local book store, you may order books directly from Mother Courage Press at 1533 Illinois Street, Racine, WI 53405. Please add $1.50 for postage and handling for the first book and $.25 for each additional book.